THE ENCYCLOPEDIA OF PSYCHOACTIVE DRUGS

IN 25 VOLUMES
Each title on a specific drug or drug-related problem

ALCOHOL
Alcohol *And Alcoholism*
Alcohol *Customs & Rituals*
Alcohol *Teenage Drinking*

HALLUCINOGENS
Flowering Plants *Magic in Bloom*
LSD *Visions or Nightmares*
Marijuana *Its Effects on Mind & Body*
Mushrooms *Psychedelic Fungi*
PCP *The Dangerous Angel*

NARCOTICS
Heroin *The Street Narcotic*
Methadone *Treatment for Addiction*
Prescription Narcotics *The Addictive Painkillers*

NON-PRESCRIPTION DRUGS
Over-the-Counter Drugs *Harmless or Hazardous?*

SEDATIVE HYPNOTICS
Barbiturates *Sleeping Potion or Intoxicant?*
Inhalants *Glue, Gas & Sniff*
Quaaludes *The Quest for Oblivion*
Valium *The Tranquil Trap*

STIMULANTS
Amphetamines *Danger in the Fast Lane*
Caffeine *The Most Popular Stimulant*
Cocaine *A New Epidemic*
Nicotine *An Old-Fashioned Addiction*

UNDERSTANDING DRUGS
The Addictive Personality
Escape from Anxiety and Stress
Getting Help *Treatments for Drug Abuse*
Treating Mental Illness
Teenage Depression and Drugs

ALCOHOL
Customs and Rituals

GENERAL EDITOR
Professor Solomon H. Snyder, M.D.
*Distinguished Service Professor of
Neuroscience, Pharmacology, and Psychiatry at
The Johns Hopkins University School of Medicine*

ASSOCIATE EDITOR
Professor Barry L. Jacobs, Ph.D.
Program in Neuroscience, Department of Psychology, Princeton University

SENIOR EDITORIAL CONSULTANT
Jerome H. Jaffe, M.D.
Director of The Addiction Research Center, National Institute on Drug Abuse

THE ENCYCLOPEDIA OF PSYCHOACTIVE DRUGS

ALCOHOL

Customs and Rituals

THOMAS BABOR, Ph.D.

Alcohol Research Center
University of Connecticut School of Medicine

1986
CHELSEA HOUSE PUBLISHERS

NEW YORK
NEW HAVEN   PHILADELPHIA

SENIOR EDITOR: William P. Hansen
ASSOCIATE EDITORS: John Haney, Richard Mandell
CAPTIONS: Thomas Babor
EDITORIAL COORDINATOR: Karyn Gullen Browne
ART DIRECTOR: Susan Lusk
LAYOUT: Carol McDougall
ART ASSISTANTS: Michael Bartz, Ghila Krajzman, Tenaz Mehta
PICTURE RESEARCH: Juliette Dickstein

COVER: Wine chalice in jasper; Florence, Italy;
Scala/Art Resource, NY

First Printing

Library of Congress Cataloging in Publication Data
Babor, Thomas.
    Alcohol, customs & rituals.
    (The Encyclopedia of psychoactive drugs)
    Bibliography: p.
    Includes index.
    Summary: Presents findings of studies done on
drinking practices of different cultures and immigrant
groups in the United States.
    1. Drinking of alcoholic beverages—Cross-cultural
studies—Juvenile literature. [1. Drinking of alcoholic
beverages—Cross-cultural studies.   2. Alcohol]
I. Title.   II. Title: Alcohol, customs and rituals.
III. Series.
HV5066.B28   1986   394.1'3   85–17466

ISBN 0-87754-763-7

Chelsea House Publishers
Harold Steinberg, Chairman & Publisher
Susan Lusk, Vice President
A Division of Chelsea House Educational Communications, Inc.

Chelsea House Publishers
133 Christopher Street
New York, NY 10014

Photos courtesy of AP/Wide World Photos; The Bettmann Archive, Inc.;
The House of Seagram; National Gallery of Art, Washington; New York
Public Library; UPI/Bettmann Newsphotos.

CONTENTS

Lucius Porter, who has been making whiskey barrels for over 52 years, is one of three such coopers left in Los Angeles. During the 3- to 12-year aging process, the oak barrel mellows and smooths the raw spirits.

FOREWORD

In the Mainstream of American Life

The rapid growth of drug use and abuse is one of the most dramatic changes in the fabric of American society in the last 20 years. The United States has the highest level of psychoactive drug use of any industrialized society. It is 10 to 30 times greater than it was 20 years ago.

According to a recent Gallup poll, young people consider drugs the leading problem that they face. One of the legacies of the social upheaval of the 1960s is that psychoactive drugs have become part of the mainstream of American life. Schools, homes, and communities cannot be "drug proofed." There is a demand for drugs—and the supply is plentiful. Social norms have changed and drugs are not only available—they are everywhere.

Almost all drug use begins in the preteen and teenage years. These years are few in the total life cycle, but critical in the maturation process. During these years adolescents face the difficult tasks of discovering their identity, clarifying their sexual roles, asserting their independence, learning to cope with authority, and searching for goals that will give their lives meaning. During this intense period of growth, conflict is inevitable and the temptation to use drugs is great. Drugs are readily available, adolescents are curious and vulnerable, there is peer pressure to experiment, and there is the temptation to escape from conflicts.

No matter what their age or socioeconomic status, no group is immune to the allure and effects of psychoactive drugs. The U.S. Surgeon General's report, "Healthy People," indicates that 30% of all deaths in the United States

Drinking customs are closely identified with the kinds of cultural artifacts sought by professional collectors such as Stephen Morris (above). Coasters, steins, posters, and a home-brewing kettle suggest beer's important role as a dietary and recreational beverage.

are premature because of alcohol and tobacco use. However, the most shocking development in this report is that mortality in the age group between 15 and 24 has increased since 1960 despite the fact that death rates for all other age groups have declined in the 20th century. Accidents, suicides, and homicides are the leading cause of death in young people 15 to 24 years of age. In many cases the deaths are directly related to drug use.

THE ENCYCLOPEDIA OF PSYCHOACTIVE DRUGS answers the questions that young people are likely to ask about drugs, as well as those they might not think to ask, but should. Topics include: what it means to be intoxicated; how drugs affect mood; why people take drugs; who takes them; when they take them; and how much they take. They will learn what happens to a drug when it enters the body. They will learn what it means to get "hooked" and how it happens. They will learn how drugs affect their driving, their schoolwork, and those around them—their peers, their family, their friends, and their employers. They will learn what the signs are that indicate that a friend or a family member may have a drug problem and to identify four stages leading from drug use to drug abuse. Myths about drugs are dispelled.

National surveys indicate that students are eager for information about drugs and that they respond to it. Students not only need information about drugs—they want information. How they get it often proves crucial. Providing young people with accurate knowledge about drugs is one of the most critical aspects.

THE ENCYCLOPEDIA OF PSYCHOACTIVE DRUGS synthesizes the wealth of new information in this field and demystifies this complex and important subject. Each volume in the series is written by an expert in the field. Handsomely illustrated, this multi-volume series is geared for teenage readers. Young people will read these books, share them, talk about them, and make more informed decisions because of them.

Miriam Cohen, Ph.D.
Contributing Editor

Ad exemplum Hrolzii
sculpsit Miller.
17 71

Obtecto dulci maerentia
Jor tristitiae, laetitiaeq.

corda lycaeo,
dator. C

C. Schonaus

Dionysus, a Greek god known to the Romans as Bacchus, was the deity of wine, dance, and ecstasy. Dionysus inspired a large following of worshipers to engage in drunken revelries during the winter and spring.

INTRODUCTION

The Gift of Wizardry
Use and Abuse

JACK H. MENDELSON, M.D.
NANCY K. MELLO, PH.D.
Alcohol and Drug Abuse Research Center
Harvard Medical School—McLean Hospital

Dorothy to the Wizard:

"I think you are a very bad man," said Dorothy.
"Oh, no, my dear; I'm really a very good man; but I'm a very bad Wizard."
—from THE WIZARD OF OZ

Man is endowed with the gift of wizardry, a talent for discovery and invention. The discovery and invention of substances that change the way we feel and behave are among man's special accomplishments, and like so many other products of our wizardry, these substances have the capacity to harm as well as to help. The substance itself is neutral, an intricate molecular structure. Yet, "too much" can be sickening, even deadly. It is man who decides how each substance is used, and it is man's beliefs and perceptions that give this neutral substance the attributes to heal or destroy.

Consider alcohol—available to all and yet regarded with intense ambivalence from biblical times to the present day. The use of alcoholic beverages dates back to our earliest ancestors. Alcohol use and misuse became associated with the worship of gods and demons. One of the most powerful Greek gods was Dionysus, lord of the Underworld and god of wine. The Romans adopted Dionysus but changed his name to Bacchus. Festivals and holidays associated with Bacchus celebrated the harvest and the origins of life. Time has blurred the images of the Bacchanalian festival, but the theme of drunkenness as a major part of celebration has survived the pagan gods and remains a familiar part of modern society. The term "Bacchanalian festival" conveys a more appealing image than "drunken orgy" or "pot

13

party," but whatever the label, some of the celebrants will inevitably start up the "high" escalator to the next plateau. Once there, the de-escalation is difficult for many.

According to reliable estimates, one out of every ten Americans develops a serious alcohol-related problem sometime in his or her lifetime. In addition, automobile accidents caused by drunken drivers claim the lives of tens of thousands every year. Many of the victims are gifted young people, just starting out in adult life. Hospital emergency rooms abound with patients seeking help for alcohol-related injuries.

Who is to blame? Can we blame the many manufacturers who produce such an amazing variety of alcoholic beverages? Should we blame the educators who fail to explain the perils of intoxication, or so exaggerate the dangers of drinking that no one could possibly believe them? Are friends to blame—those peers who urge others to "drink more and faster," or the macho types who stress the importance of being able to "hold your liquor"? Casting blame, however, is hardly constructive, and pointing the finger is a fruitless way to deal with problems. Alcoholism and drug abuse have few culprits but many victims. Accountability begins with each of us, every time we choose to use or to misuse an intoxicating substance.

It is ironic that some of man's earliest medicines, derived from natural plant products, are used today to poison and to intoxicate. Relief from pain and suffering is one of society's many continuing goals. Over 3,000 years ago, the Therapeutic Papyrus of Thebes, one of our earliest written records, gave instructions for the use of opium in the treatment of pain. Opium, in the form of its major derivative, morphine, remains one of the most powerful drugs we have for pain relief. But opium, morphine, and similar compounds, such as heroin, have also been used by many to induce changes in mood and feeling. Another example of man's misuse of a natural substance is the coca leaf, which for centuries was used by the Indians of Peru to reduce fatigue and hunger. Its modern derivative, cocaine, has important medical use as a local anesthetic. Unfortunately, its increasing abuse in the 1980s has reached epidemic proportions.

The purpose of this series is to provide information about the nature and behavioral effects of alcohol and drugs, and the probable consequences of both their moderate use and abuse. The authors believe that up-to-date, objective information about alcohol and drugs will help readers make better decisions as to whether to use them or not. The information presented here (and in other books in this series) is based on many clinical and laboratory studies and observations by people from diverse walks of life.

Over the centuries, novelists, poets, and dramatists have provided us with many insights into the beneficial and problematic aspects of alcohol and drug use. Physicians, lawyers, biologists, psychologists, and social scientists have contributed to a better understanding of the causes and consequences of using these substances. The authors in this series have attempted to gather and condense all the latest information about drug use and abuse. They have also described the sometimes wide gaps in our knowledge and have suggested some new ways to answer many difficult questions.

One such question, for example, is how do alcohol and drug problems get started? And what is the best way to treat them when they do? Not too many years ago, alcoholics and drug abusers were regarded as evil, immoral, or both. It is now recognized that these persons suffer from very complicated diseases involving deep psychological and social problems. To understand how the disease begins and progresses, it is necessary to understand the nature of the substance, the behavior of the afflicted person, and the characteristics of the society or culture in which he lives.

The diagram below shows the interaction of these three factors. The arrows indicate that the substance not only affects the user personally, but the society as well. Society influences attitudes towards the substance, which in turn affect its availability. The substance's impact upon the society may support or discourage the use and abuse of that substance.

SUBSTANCE
(ALCOHOL OR DRUG)

PERSON ⟷ SOCIETY

Although many of the social environments we live in are very similar, some of the most subtle differences can strongly influence our thinking and behavior. Where we live, go to school and work, whom we discuss things with—all influence our opinions about drug use and misuse. Yet we also share certain commonly accepted beliefs that outweigh any differences in our attitudes. The authors in this series have tried to identify and discuss the central, most crucial issues concerning drug use and misuse.

Regrettably, man's wizardry in developing new substances in medical therapeutics has not always been paralleled by intelligent usage. Although we do know a great deal about the effects of alcohol and drugs, we have yet to learn how to impart that knowledge, especially to young adults.

Does it matter? What harm does it do to smoke a little pot or have a few beers? What is it like to be intoxicated? How long does it last? Will it make me feel really fine? Will it make me sick? What are the risks? These are but a few of the questions answered in this series, which, hopefully, will enable the reader to make wise decisions concerning the crucial issue of drugs.

Information sensibly acted upon can go a long way towards helping everyone develop his or her best self. As one keen and sensitive observer, Dr. Lewis Thomas, has said,

> "There is nothing at all absurd about the human condition. We matter. It seems to me a good guess, hazarded by a good many people who have thought about it, that we may be engaged in the formation of something like a mind for the life of this planet. If this is so, we are still at the most primitive stage, still fumbling with language and thinking, but infinitely capacitated for the future. Looked at this way, it is remarkable that we've come as far as we have in so short a period, really no time at all as geologists measure time. We are the newest, the youngest, and the brightest thing around."

***Three aspects of the New York City Bowery reflected in a store window:
homelessness, alcoholism, and unemployment. Even these men follow
a certain set of drinking customs passed from one generation to the next.***

Civic pride and ethnic tradition produce a spontaneous celebration by Milwaukee Braves fans in 1957. Drinking is a part of the informal social rules that serve as a guide to everyday behavior for these descendants of German and Scandinavian immigrants who naturally fill their steins with beer to express their joy.

AUTHOR'S PREFACE

When friendly discussion turns to the subject of alcohol, it is common to hear boastful comparisons about the drinking customs of different ethnic, religious, or national groups. Common belief holds that people of Irish descent drink more than those of non-Irish descent, American Indians more than descendants of European immigrants, and Catholics more than Protestants. This book draws on both historical evidence and recent international statistics to show how social customs and rituals to a large extent shape the way people drink.

Drinking habits commonly grow from the traditions of a specific community of people. This means that, over time, the uses and functions of alcohol have become guided by generally accepted rules and regulations that specify who drinks, what and how much is consumed, and how the drinker should behave. One example of these traditional practices that is common to almost all societies is ceremonial drinking, such as that which takes place at weddings and formal banquets. On these occasions social custom dictates that a special alcoholic beverage, such as champagne, be consumed after a toast is offered to the guests of honor. On less formal occasions, drinking customs specify what beverages are offered to a visitor or ordered at a restaurant.

Custom also plays an important role in determining when and where people get drunk and how they behave under the influence of alcohol. Cocktail parties are occasions for copious drinking, but excessive drunkenness is considered inappropriate. Fraternity parties, on the other hand, are occasions when intoxication and wild behavior are acceptable—even expected.

In contrast to social drinking customs, religious rituals often incorporate the use of alcohol in a way that sanctifies both the beverage and the process of drinking. The *kiddush* is a Jewish ritual performed at festivals and holy days, such as the Sabbath. Participants typically read prayers that declare the sanctity of the occasion, perform a blessing over a cupful of wine, and then share the wine. In Christian churches, the celebration of the Lord's Supper, or Eucharist, includes the drinking of wine.

The tremendous diversity in drinking customs is indicated in Table 1. The survey data reveal very strikingly the huge variation in alcohol consumption among the various nations of the world and the overwhelming concentration of heavy drinking in Europe. Nine of the first ten rankings are held by European countries. The nations of Africa and the Middle East report the lowest per person consumption. The United States ranks 19th on the list.

Also interesting is the tremendous difference among nations in beverage preferences. The people of France, Italy, Portugal, Spain, Greece, Argentina, and Chile are predominantly wine drinkers. In the Netherlands, Ireland, Great Britain, Australia, Canada, and Mexico the preferred alcoholic beverage is beer. In contrast, Iceland, Poland, Sweden, and the Soviet Union, as well as Peru, Bolivia, and Cuba tend to use distilled spirits. A few countries, such as Switzerland and Japan, divide their drinking equally among several beverages. Although many people believe the United States is a liquor-drinking nation, beer has been the most popular beverage since the Civil War.

In general, the countries with a high rate of wine drinking also have the highest total consumption, and the countries with a high rate of spirits drinking have the lowest. (Here consumption of an alcoholic beverage refers to the relative proportion of absolute alcohol consumed, not the total volume of liquid. Beers average 4.5% alcohol, wines about 12%, and straight spirits approximately 40%. Therefore, 12 ounces of beer, one glass, or 4 to 5 ounces, of wine, and a shot, or 1.5 ounces, of spirits all contain approximately .6 ounces of alcohol.) Developing countries tend to have lower drinking rates than industrialized nations, although consumption in almost all nations of the world has increased since 1960.

The differences in consumption between ethnic and religious groups within countries are often just as great as the differences among nations. What accounts for these variations in the amount and types of alcohol consumed? The following chapters will show how historical circumstances and cultural influences shape drinking customs and how drinking customs in turn prescribe how, why, where, and when alcoholic beverages are used.

Young and old come together to mark the observance of the Jewish holiday of Passover, which commemorates the exodus from Egypt. This holiday, rich in symbolism, uses both ceremonial foods and wine.

During the Roman Empire, heavy drinking, exemplified by such emperors as Nero and Caligula, was commonplace.

CHAPTER 1

DRINKING THROUGHOUT THE AGES

*T*he drinking customs and rituals of any given nation are intimately associated with its historical and cultural development. Geography, economics, politics, religion, and ethnic diversity also play a part. Since alcoholic beverages have been used in nearly every part of the world since ancient times, any historical survey of drinking customs must begin with the birth of civilization in the Middle East.

The Middle East

Records of ancient civilizations give evidence of the use of alcoholic beverages as long ago as 6000 B.C.E. (*Note*: B.C.E., Before the Common Era, is equivalent to B.C.) Wine making is believed to have originated in the Middle East, where wild grapevines produce an abundance of fruit without any cultivation. Because fermentation occurs naturally when fruits and other substances are exposed to air, wine and beer making and agriculture probably developed concurrently. The Old Testament credits Noah with planting the first vineyard on Mt. Ararat in present-day Turkey, and notes that he was the first person to experience drunkenness.

From the earliest times alcohol has had various functions. In the Sumerian city of Nippur beer and wine were used for medicinal purposes as early as 2000 B.C.E. Ancient Egyptian and Assyrian religious and festive occasions included drinking bouts that often lasted for several days. Osiris, one of Egypt's most popular gods, perhaps was held in such high esteem because of his reputation for having been the first to cultivate the grapevine and to manufacture beer from grain.

The tomb of an Egyptian king who lived approximately 5,000 years ago bears what could be interpreted as the first known epitaph to an alcoholic: "His earthly abode was rent and shattered by wine and beer. And the spirit escaped before it was called for." And well before that time Egypt had developed an organized wine industry, which included a network of vineyards, taverns, and trade routes. Most drinking tended to take place at social and religious festivals, though among the rich, banquets were frequently occasions for excessive drinking.

The Greeks

The first alcoholic beverage to gain widespread popularity on the Hellenic peninsula was mead, a fermented drink made from honey and water. By 1700 B.C.E. Greek civilization had attained a level of development sufficient to make

In this 18th-century engraving of people waiting for the Flood, God's punishment is contrasted with intoxication, sensuality, and gluttony. After the Jews' liberation from Egypt, wine use was strictly controlled.

locally-produced wine commonplace, and during the next thousand years wine drinking took on the same functions later found in many other cultures. Firstly, alcohol was incorporated into religious rituals, especially as an offering to the dead and to the gods. Secondly, drinking became part of hospitality customs and was often used as an intoxicant at formal banquets and informal social gatherings. Thirdly, wine was employed as a medicine for healing and for the relief of pain. Lastly, dietary uses were developed, making wine a integral part of daily meals.

Habitual drunkenness was uncommon in ancient Greece, perhaps because moderation in all things, including drinking, was an important ideal in Greek society. The cult of Dionysus, a minor god reputed to have brought the grapevine to the Greeks, was an exception to this ideal. By the 7th century B.C.E. wine production had become a part of

Osiris, one of ancient Egypt's most popular gods, presides over the "Court of Death" that guided people to the other world. The Egyptians credited Osiris with bringing the gift of wine, which was as popular as this god until the 7th century C.E., when Islam became the dominant religion.

Greek agriculture. With good wine readily available, drinking began to play a more important part in daily life. About this time Dionysus became identified with mystical rituals that included music, dancing, intoxication and, at times, even bloody human sacrifice. These revelries were viewed with growing concern by Greek leaders. Some cities succeeded in controlling these rituals by introducing publicly sponsored drinking holidays, but in the process festival drinking became institutionalized.

The symposium, a gathering of men for an evening of conversation, entertainment, and drinking, played an important part in Greek culture. The evening usually began with a banquet and invariably ended with drunkenness. When the wine was first served, a small quantity was poured out as a libation to the "good spirit." Then the guests drank to the health of each other by passing a cup from person to person.

Bacchus, who initially took the form of a beast or a bearded man, was later given soft, youthful, feminine, or even infant-like qualities.

This was sometimes followed by competitive drinking bouts in which the master of the symposium determined the order and quantity of drinking.

Philosophers such as Socrates and Plato counseled temperance and spoke out against the growing incidence of drunkenness in Athens. However, their advice was not followed by the greatest Greek warrior of all, Alexander the Great, whose bouts of drinking after victories became legendary. His mother was a devotee of the Dionysian philosophy and his father, King Philip of Macedon, was notorious for his drunkenness at festival times. From many accounts Alexander's drinking bouts were often marred by violence, and there is evidence that his last alcoholic binge may have contributed to his untimely death at age 33.

Drinking figured prominently in the short but brilliant career of Alexander the Great. Several years after the festival pictured here that honored his son's birth, Alexander died from a drunken binge. Like the people of most ancient civilizations, the Greeks developed elaborate drinking customs to accompany important occasions.

The Hebrews

The Hebrews were first introduced to wine during their captivity in Egypt. When Moses led his people to Palestine around 1200 B.C.E., the Hebrew people found that the area was already rich in vineyards. As the new settlers became established in the towns and cities of Palestine, their drinking habits began to be criticized by the Rechabites and Nazarites, conservative groups who practiced abstinence from alcohol. Hostility to wine, and especially to drunkenness, is particularly evident in many Old Testament stories. Noah's drunkenness and shame resulted from his planting of the vine. And the Book of Proverbs condemned the "love of wine" because it led to arguments, poverty, and madness.

When in 586 B.C.E. the Hebrews were conquered by the Babylonians, they were deported to a city noted for its excessive use of alcohol. In fact, widespread drunkenness

Noah, pictured in a 15th-century woodcut, is credited with being the first to plant the grapevine and produce wine. During a drunken sleep, Noah's naked body was seen by his son Ham, whose descendants were cursed.

may have led to Babylon's downfall—in 539 B.C.E. the Persians attacked and captured the Babylonians while they were drunk and in the midst of a festival.

With the return of the Hebrews, now called Jews, to Palestine following the Exile, their drinking habits and attitudes toward alcohol became more moderate in tone. Over the next two centuries wine drinking was integrated into many religious ceremonies, becoming a symbol of the sanctification of the Sabbath and of other Jewish holy days. At the same time that dietary and ceremonial drinking became widely accepted, there was an increase in sobriety.

Detailed regulations concerning the proper use of wine were written into the Talmud and other holy books. Phrases such as this one gave special emphasis to the evils of drunkenness: "Be not drunk with wine; for wine turneth the mind from the truth, and inspires the passion of lust, and leadeth the eyes into error. . . ."

The Romans

Viticulture, the cultivation of vines, was probably first introduced to the Italian peninsula by Greek settlers. From the founding of Rome in 753 B.C.E. until the 3rd century B.C.E., Roman vineyards were small and wine was insufficiently available to make regular drinking possible on a wide scale. After the Roman conquest of Italy and the entire Mediterranean basin, the traditional Roman values of frugality, simplicity, and temperance were gradually replaced by ambition, corruption, and hard drinking. As a result, viticulture assumed a major role in the agricultural economy, making good wine abundant and inexpensive. About this time the Dionysian rites spread to Italy. The Bacchanalia, as these rites were called in Latin, were characterized not only by excessive eating and drinking, but often by sexual promiscuity, bizarre religious ceremonies, and ritualistic murders. Although the Roman senate tried to ban the Bacchanalia in 186 B.C.E., they were later revived in the 1st century C.E. (C.E. is equivalent to A.D.) under the emperors Caligula and Claudius, who encouraged them to the point of furnishing festival wines at public expense.

By the 1st century B.C.E. wine had become Rome's most popular beverage as well as a major export item and an important source of government revenue. As Rome attracted a huge population of displaced persons from rural Italy and other parts of the empire, wine was distributed free or sold at cost. Whereas heavy drinking had previously been limited to festival periods, excessive daily drinking now became widespread, prevalent even among the increasingly decadent upper class.

At the height of the Roman Empire the economic fortunes of Italy came to depend to a great extent on its vineyards. Not only had wine become the most important domestic industry, but concerted efforts were made to expand its sale and use beyond the peninsula. Thus, the Roman conquests of northern Europe brought sophisticated methods of viticulture to France, Germany, Spain, and the British Isles. However, contemporary writers continued to lament the excessive drinking habits of their fellow Romans, especially those of the members of the ruling class. As luxury, avarice, greed, and ambition ushered in the decline of Rome,

The grapevine could not be cultivated on a large scale until the development of the grape knife, a simple and ancient instrument that is still used today. Its curved tip and short blade are ideal for clipping grape clusters without bruising the fruit.

heavy drinking was often implicated as a cause of many social ills.

The shift from ceremonial drinking—confined to banquets and special occasions—to casual, everyday drinking was accompanied by an increase in chronic drunkenness, which today would be labeled alcoholism. The Emperor Tiberius, who reigned from 14 to 37 C.E., was described as a lonely and depressed alcoholic. The drunken escapades of

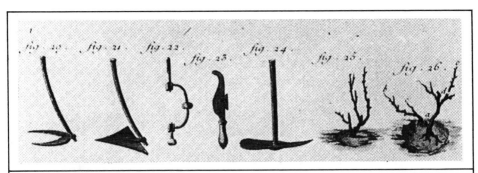

Monks created a variety of special tools to cultivate the wine grape. Modifications of the hoe and two methods of grafting are illustrated above. Climate and soil conditions greatly affect the quality of grapes.

Caligula, who succeeded him, led to his assassination as he was leaving the games in the arena. Claudius was said to have rarely left the dinner room sober. The notorious Nero, emperor from 54 to 69 C.E., haunted the taverns, caroused in the streets, and staged extravagant revels. So many holidays were introduced under Nero (159 by one count) that drinking at festivals became a major pastime of unemployed Romans.

Roman customs that fostered heavy alcohol consumption included drinking before meals on an empty stomach; using a feather to induce vomiting so that more wine and food could be consumed; and guzzling as many cups as indicated by the throw of the dice, one of the Romans' many wine-drinking games.

Following the death of Nero, the level of drunkenness among the imperial court seems to have declined. The spread of Christianity may have assisted the return to moderation among the wealthy and the poor. The Roman emperor Domitian's enforcement of a program that reduced the number of vineyards to prevent overproduction, raised the price of wine, and thus stabilized the wine industry, may have been another factor that furthered the return to sobriety.

When Jesus used wine to symbolize his blood at the Last Supper, illustrated above in Leonardo da Vinci's painting, he endowed the drink with a mystical quality. Since then wine has been an integral part of Christian rituals.

The Early Christians and Medieval Europeans

As Christianity replaced the pagan religions of Greece and Rome, the drinking customs of Western Europe began to be influenced by the earliest New Testament writings. One of these scriptures relates the story of the marriage feast of Cana at which Jesus changed water into wine. And at the Last Supper, Jesus used wine as the symbol of his blood. Both Jesus and St. Paul condemned drunkenness and expected sobriety on the part of their disciples. By the 3rd century, however, festival drinking in commemoration of Christian martyrs had become popular.

In the early part of the Middle Ages (500–1000), the Celts and Germans drank beer and cider, though their primitive living conditions did not allow them the luxury of drinking to excess. Similarly, the peoples of the Romance countries (present-day Italy, Spain, and France) drank light wine. The inhabitants of the British Isles drank ale, beer, and mead. In medieval as in Roman times, periodic binge drinking during festivals was common.

During the Middle Ages alcoholic beverages were, for the most part, produced locally. With the collapse of the Roman Empire religious institutions, particularly the monasteries, became the repositories of the brewing and wine-making techniques developed in the ancient world. In addition to making wine to celebrate the Christian Mass, the monks produced large quantities of wine to support the maintenance and expansion of the monastic movement. It was the monks who saved viticulture during the barbarian invasions that destroyed many other facets of the Roman Empire. Throughout the early Middle Ages only the monks had the stability, security, and economic resources to conduct large-scale viticulture and thereby to improve the quality of their wines. For nearly 1,300 years, the largest and the best vineyards were owned and managed by religious orders.

In France monks developed the burgundies, bordeaux, and champagnes that graced the finest tables of the medieval chateaux. In Germany they created moselle and rhine wines. The abbeys of Austria, Italy, Spain, Switzerland, Portugal, and Hungary all cultivated the grape. The California wine industry also was begun by Franciscan monks who established the first missions there in the 1700s.

Monks perfected the art of sparkling champagne by introducing the bottle cork. This invention allowed them to exploit the second fermentation and to age their wines properly in bottles. Monastic orders were probably the first to fortify sherry, and to bring the technology of distillation to widespread use on the European continent. The monastery names on wine labels still confer an aura of reverence, a legacy of the time when the church held a virtual monopoly on the cultivation of the grape and the production and distribution of both wine and spirits.

If alcohol became the curse of the ruling classes in Rome, it became the curse of the religious class in the

During the early Middle Ages the science of distillation was kept alive in the European monastaries. The use of aqua vitae (water of life), made from herbs, plants, and spices, developed into the production of flavored liqueurs.

Middle Ages. Clerical drinking was common not only at meals, where fine wine became an important means of impressing visitors and pilgrims, but also during the numerous religious festivals. By the late Middle Ages monks were typically portrayed in poetry and fiction as jovial, fun-loving, and hard-drinking. Periodically, church officials and secular rulers found it necessary to impose penalties and regulations on the use of alcohol by clerics.

Western drinking customs were further developed during the 12th and 13th centuries as tremendous changes occurred in agriculture, trade, and population. Although distillation of liquors probably originated in the Greco-Roman era, it was introduced to Europe only around 1250, and beverages with high alcohol content did not become popular until the 1700s. With the development of trade routes to and from the southern wine-producing countries, wine consumption increased in England and the Low Countries. In the early 14th century hopped-beer brewing became established in such northern lands as England, Netherlands, Germany, Poland, and Russia, and beer became the national beverage of many of these countries.

Accompanying the establishment of national beverage preferences was the development of numerous drinking customs and rituals that, while similar to those common in ancient and Greco-Roman civilizations, went far beyond them in number and complexity.

Following the discovery of distillation, spirits drinking became associated with a number of religious rituals and medical customs. Early manuscripts carefully transcribed by monks couched the process of distillation in mystery. Spirits were first produced on a small scale and sold as costly medicines by monks, physicians, and apothecaries. Initially, spirits were distilled by burning off the alcohol from already fermented wine, hence the name *bernenwijn* ("burnt wine"), or brandy. Arnald of Villanova, a French professor of medicine, called distilled spirits *aqua vitae* (water of life) because it "strengthens the body and prolongs life." In a widely read treatise he encouraged the medicinal use of wine and spirits. He even praised the therapeutic value of periodic intoxication (up to two times a month), which purges the body of "noxious humours." Medicinal uses of wine and spirits were numerous: as a prophylactic against the plague, an analgesic for pain, an adjunct to health in damp and cold climates, and an energy booster during manual labor.

By the 16th century brandy had become a popular recreational drink in Germany. With the improved taste of flavored liqueurs introduced about the same time in France, these drinks became a favorite of the aristocracy as an after-dinner drink.

Perhaps no other institution was more responsible for the spread of drinking customs and habits than the tavern. Taverns had been important social institutions at least since the time of the ancient Greeks, and their reemergence in the cities and towns of Europe began with the growing availability of alcoholic beverages. Taverns and cabarets became the centers of social and intellectual life of European medieval cities. They were places where one could enjoy the company of old friends, make new friends, and/or be by

A meeting of wandering minstrels in medieval England. Drinking was a popular theme of poets and songwriters who often met in taverns and inns.

oneself. Celebrated in song and poetry, these establishments became places where heavy drinking and intoxication were tolerated and, at times, encouraged.

In the 12th and 13th centuries wandering minstrels, students, and poets popularized uproarious drinking songs that embodied youthful revolt against the rigidity of the conventional medieval world. As the tavern became a place to celebrate the joys of wine, it is not surprising that it was periodically condemned as "sinful and utterly unlawful unto Christians."

Modern Europe

By the beginning of the 17th century travelers who described the drinking habits of the different European countries were already depicting scenes similar to those of the present day. In 1618 English traveler Gynes Moryson noted that the English were moderate drinkers who "at a feast will drinke two or three healths in remembrance of speciall friends, or respected honourable persons but in generall the greater and better part of the English, hold all excess blameworthy, and drunkenness a reprochfull vice." Even more temperate than the English are the French who "drinke water mingled with wine." In contrast, Moryson found the Germans, Irish, and Scots to be excessive drinkers. He reported that the Germans indulged in beer, wine, and brandies as excessively as they ate food, and noted that the Irish drank heavily on marketing days when both men and women would get drunk on wine and whiskey in the towns.

Throughout Europe from 1600 to 1750 there was a tremendous increase in the consumption of beer, wine, brandies, and liqueurs. Improvements in agriculture, better methods of brewing, and new technologies for distillation of spirits were, in part, responsible for the increase in drinking by both peasants and city dwellers. For perhaps the first time since the decline of the Roman Empire, habitual drinking among large segments of the population, particularly the lower classes, became a major social problem in large cities.

Although brandy was used extensively as a medicine and tonic, it did not gain popularity as a beverage throughout Europe. This honor was reserved for whiskey, a word derived from *uisge beathe*, the Irish-Gaelic equivalent of *aqua vitae.* The Irish reputation for heavy drinking came from alcohol's special role in their diet. They have also used it as an all-purpose medicine, and even as a major form of currency. The Irish are thought to have been the first people to use alcohol to treat hangovers, a cure often associated with the expression "the hair of the dog that bit you." The primary social use of alcohol by the Irish was to induce conviviality at christenings and wakes. Often held at night in graveyards, these occasions were characterized by heavy drinking and even fights between opposing family factions.

Because of the harsh taste of the whiskeys of Ireland and Scotland, gin became the preferred type of distilled beverage throughout the rest of Europe. This beverage was first introduced in 1672 by the Dutch, who added juniper berries to Scottish grain alcohol to make it. The French called it *ginevere*, but British soldiers returning from wars in the Low Countries shortened its name to gin. When Britain's William III barred the importation of French wines and

A hardworking vintner raises a glass of wine to test its clarity. Accompanying this late 18th-century etching was a poem which concluded with the thought that for a man whose god presides over the expansive vineyards, the barrel becomes a temple of holiness.

brandies, the people were encouraged to substitute domestic gin. A favorable tax policy, coupled with population shifts brought on by the Industrial Revolution, led to the multiplication of distilleries and the proliferation of pubs. Cheap liquor was sold everywhere in London and in lieu of wages was given by employers to laborers. As a result there was a great increase in the drinking of spirits between 1720 and 1751, a period plagued by what is known as the gin epidemic.

The gin epidemic, coupled with the social disruption created by the Industrial Revolution, was seen as the cause of poverty, vice, drunkenness, and the high mortality rate among the urban poor. The depravity of London's poor was described graphically in William Hogarth's popular etching "Gin Lane." It shows a gin shop advertised by a sign reading: "drunk for a penny, dead drunk for twopence, clean straw for nothing." In contrast, Hogarth's "Beer Street" presents an idealized picture of prosperous, happy, overfed

This 1779 depiction of an English "stag" party suggests that some drinking customs have changed little over the centuries.

ale drinkers. The lesson was not lost on the English. Mobilized by the religious fervor of Methodism and by the growing concern for the health and safety of industrial workers, the movement to impose strict controls on the gin trade gained strength. As a result, the English gradually switched their drinking habits to beer.

A 1751 engraving by William Hogarth, entitled Gin Lane, *depicts the conspicuous drinking of cheap liquor by London's lower classes.*

One exception to this trend toward moderation was the custom of giving a daily ration of rum or brandy to soldiers and sailors. This allotment of alcohol to soldiers had been a common practice since ancient times. The rum ration, as well as the other ceremonial drinking rituals associated with it, played a prominent role in the birth of modern Australia. On January 26, 1788, British governor Arthur Phillip landed at Sydney Cove with his red-coated marines, raised the Union Jack over the new colony, and drank to the health of King George III. Ten days later 600 male convicts whom Phillip had brought from England to settle the new land gave thanks in their own way. The arrival of 200 convict women at the same time that extra rum rations were being issued led to a "scene of Debauchery and Riot." Though soaked by a violent thunderstorm, the convicts brawled and drank until they dropped.

Alcoholism was especially prevalent in the upper classes of Europe. In 18th-century France the boredom of court life was relieved by wild parties, during which drunkenness was

In contrast to Gin Lane, *which illustrated the evils of the gin epidemic in England between 1720 and 1751, in* Beer Street *Hogarth painted an idealized picture of happy, prosperous, overfed ale drinkers.*

common even among women. In Russia, heavy drinking was promoted by the example of Czar Peter the Great (1682–1725), who often joined his drunken friends on the streets of Moscow for an evening of carousing and singing bawdy songs. At state banquets, he insisted that guests drink until they got sick or passed out.

It was not until the 19th century that the production of beer, wine, and distilled beverages became efficient and cheap enough to supply inexpensive alcohol to the masses. With the emergence of the modern nation-state in Europe, the one social problem practically every country shared was alcoholism, as reflected in records of public drunkenness, industrial accidents, and hospitalization for "insanity caused by intemperance." In the Scandinavian countries heavy aquavit drinking caused widespread drunkenness. In France the urban working classes lived in squalor while squandering their wages on cheap brandy and a hallucinogenic liquor called absinthe. Distilled from toxic wormwood oil, absinthe became the favorite drink of the artists and writers of Paris.

ANOTHER IMPORTED FASHION.

This 19th-century editorial cartoon portrays the real and imagined evils of absinthe, a popular and potent liqueur that was the rage of Paris during the Gay Nineties despite its supposed link with murders, suicides, and insanity. When consumed in large quantities, absinthe reputedly produced convulsions, hallucinations, and brain damage.

As drinking and alcohol problems increased dramatically in almost every industrialized country, groups of clerics, business leaders, physicians, and social reformers took up the challenge to curb the alcoholic beverage industry. First begun in the United States in the early 1800s, the temperance movement quickly spread to Europe. In most countries, the temperance movement was successful in changing public attitudes and passing laws to control the production of alcoholic beverages. In the late 19th century, the European countries agreed to limit the spread of distilled beverages to their African colonies.

On the eve of World War I alcohol was considered a sufficient enough threat to society that laws prohibiting its manufacture and sale were enacted in the United States, Finland, Belgium, Iceland, Norway, England, and Russia. However, by the 1930s, most of these laws had been repealed, partly because the alcohol problems they were designed to deal with were no longer apparent to the new generation of drinkers who came of age between the World Wars.

Carrying placards protesting the use of alcohol, children of the Soviet Union participate in a 1930s anti-liquor demonstration in Moscow.

Outside America's oldest winery in New York, casks dry after repairs.
Spanish missionaries brought viticulture to the United States in the 1700s.

CHAPTER 2

DRINKING
IN THE UNITED STATES

*T*he first European settlers on the North American continent brought with them a great variety of drinking customs and beverage preferences. Despite the religious orthodoxy of the Puritans and Quakers, it appears that the new colonists indulged themselves more freely in the New World than in the Old.

Until the 19th century cider was the most common beverage in the colonies. It was produced in abundance from the apple orchards that dotted the landscapes of New England and New York. Cider was stored in barrels in farm cellars so that the natural process of fermentation could produce a mild alcoholic apple wine that lasted throughout the year. Provided liberally to every member of the family, cider was served at breakfast, dinner, and supper, was consumed in the fields between meals, and was a regular staple at all social functions. Though its popularity was often overshadowed by the more exotic cocktails and distilled beverages that came into vogue during the 1700s, it is likely that cider was America's national beverage until the early 19th century.

Other fruits used to make mildly alcoholic wines were pears, strawberries, elderberries, and grapes. Honey, which like apples was also harvested in abundance in New York and New England, was fermented into mead using ancient recipes. The mead was then doctored with herbs and spices to produce a drink called Old Methaglin. Beer, brewed locally where hops could be grown, was another important beverage, although its popularity never rivaled that of cider, rum, or whiskey until after the Civil War. Portuguese fortified wines such as Madeira and port were also popular in the colonies, but only the wealthier classes could afford to use them in quantity.

Shortly after 1650, trade with Barbados in the West Indies began, a development that was to have a profound effect on colonial drinking patterns. Molasses and sugar cane, imported by New England traders, provided the raw material for rum production. Cheaper than the rum made in the islands, it soon became one of the most popular beverages in the colonies. It was often consumed in the form of mixed drinks such as punch and flip. Flip was a winter favorite made from rum and beer, sweetened with sugar, and warmed by plunging a red hot fireplace poker into the mug in which it was served.

Temperance reformers flooded the country with pamphlets like this one depicting spirits as the cause of violence, disease, and insanity.

Contrary to the stereotype of the stern Puritan and the stoical Quaker, the majority of the colonialists considered alcoholic beverages necessary and beneficial. Drinking, later to be condemned by the Puritans' descendants as "Demon Rum," was praised by Increase Mather in 1673 as "a good creature of God." An important distinction was made between drinking and drunkenness: "The wine is from God, but the drunkard is from the Devil."

Intoxication was sometimes treated with severe punishment. Habitual drunkards were sometimes whipped or forced to wear a mark of shame. And once so labeled they were refused the right to purchase liquor. During the 17th century each colony specified a fine or prescribed the stocks for the first offense of drunkenness. Repeated offenders could receive hard labor or corporal punishment.

Given the widespread availability and use of alcoholic beverages, the general sobriety of the first colonies is nota-

One of the most dramatic symptoms of advanced alcoholism is delirium tremens. Often illustrated in temperance pamphlets to discourage drinking, DTs are characterized by tremulousness, disorientation, agitation, fever, and frightening hallucinations. Before modern medicine, many alcoholics died of DTs while drying out in jail cells.

ble. In all likelihood it was only the strict sanctions against blatant intoxication, the disciplined colonial lifestyle, and the close-knit nature of colonial towns that prevented the development of more serious drinking problems.

By the 18th century, however, colonial drinking customs had begun to change. Increasing affluence made domestic rum and foreign wine more affordable. And the erosion of traditional values removed the moral stigma once associated with acute intoxication.

Following the development of domestic distillation in 1684, the rum industry grew dramatically in Boston, Newport, and Providence. Almost every important town from Massachusetts to the Carolinas possessed a still to meet the local demand. After 1730 distilled liquor became a key component of the Triangle Trade, a commercial network in which New England rum was exchanged for West African slaves, who in turn were sold for West Indian molasses. Some of

An illicit whiskey still in the mountains is surprised by revenue officers. In 1794 thousands of farmers refused to pay the whiskey tax, but when federal troops were called out the Whiskey Rebellion soon ended.

the distilled rum was shipped to Africa and the rest was sold and consumed locally. By the eve of the Revolution the liquor trade was a significant and profitable part of both domestic and foreign commerce.

One consequence of the rapid expansion of the liquor industry was that drinking penetrated into almost every aspect of colonial social life. Readily available at homes, inns, and retail stores, liquor was copiously imbibed at work, at meals, and during leisure time. In sickness, liquor became a common medicine prescribed by every colonial physician. In health, spirits were believed to be a useful source of energy. In fact, manual workers were typically provided with a free daily ration of rum as a fringe benefit of their employment. Communal gatherings such as weddings, house raisings, or the ordination of a minister were further occasions for the liberal provision of cider, punch, and rum. Social drinking was often a part of daily business at meetings of the town selectmen, local merchants, or colonial militia.

Given the pervasive use of alcohol throughout the American colonies, it is not surprising that alcohol-related problems did develop. In sermons, pamphlets, diaries, and newspaper articles, New Englanders noted with alarm the decline in personal conduct and public morals associated with increased liquor consumption. Puritan minister Cotton Mather, whose father had called wine the good creature of God, expressed his fear that "the flood of excessive drinking" was about to "drown Christianity." Yet another cause of concern was the growing production of whiskey in the frontier settlements beyond the Appalachians.

Temperance Reform

By 1790 alcohol consumption had attained an estimated annual level of nearly six gallons of pure alcohol per person, more than two times the current level of consumption (see Figure 1). At the turn of the century distilled spirits for the first time surpassed cider and other fermented beverages as America's favorite type of alcoholic drink. The national binge continued into the 1830s when support for sobriety abruptly sprang up in America in the form of one of the most powerful social movements in the country's history—the American temperance movement.

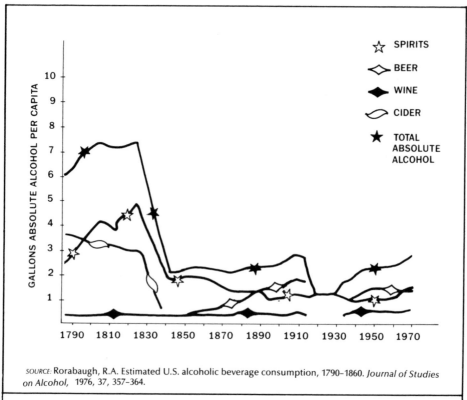

SOURCE: Rorabaugh, R.A. Estimated U.S. alcoholic beverage consumption, 1790–1860. *Journal of Studies on Alcohol,* 1976, 37, 357–364.

Figure 1. *U.S. per capita consumption of alcobolic beverages and absolute alcobol between 1790 and 1970.*

The father of the temperance movement was Dr. Benjamin Rush, one of the first to label intemperance a disease. In 1784 he published "An inquiry into the Effects of Ardent Spirits Upon the Human Minde and Body." In it he advocated a plan of action which served as a blueprint for temperance reform: active involvement of church leaders, petitions to limit the number of taverns, heavy taxes on liquor, and consistent sanctions against public intoxication. Rush's pamphlet served as the foundation of the first temperance organizations, which grew dramatically during the 1820s and 1830s. Their members met regularly to plan action, pledging to abstain from liquor or, in some cases, all alcoholic beverages.

With the strong involvement of the nation's Protestant churches, the "temperance crusade" took on many of the characteristics of a religious revival. Temperance was preached as a logical corollary to the gospel, and by 1835 more than 35,000 ministers had shown their support for it by signing the pledge of abstinence.

By organizing large numbers of energetic, middle-class men and women into locally-based volunteer interest groups, temperance reformers were able to apply pressure directly on the political process. Exploiting the power of the printed word, a massive propaganda campaign was carried out through the distribution of millions of cheap temperance tracts. By 1855 membership had surpassed 1,000,000 and included men, women, and children.

The most striking result of this campaign was the dramatic change in per capita alcohol consumption that began about 1830 (see Figure 1). Consumption of both liquor and

In the 1880s the temperance movement attracted large numbers of women and thus provided a training ground for women's rights activists. Motivated by a genuine concern for family stability, they sometimes protested by singing hymns in front of the "drunkard making" saloons.

A MORAL AND PHYSICAL THERMOMETER.

A scale of the progress of Temperance and Intemperance.—Liquors with effects in their usual order.

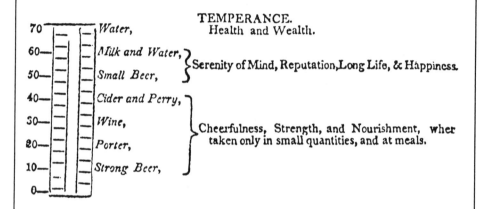

TEMPERANCE.
Health and Wealth.

70 — Water,	
60 — Milk and Water,	}Serenity of Mind, Reputation, Long Life, & Happiness.
50 — Small Beer,	
40 — Cider and Perry,	
30 — Wine,	}Cheerfulness, Strength, and Nourishment, when taken only in small quantities, and at meals.
20 — Porter,	
10 — Strong Beer,	
0 —	

INTEMPERANCE.

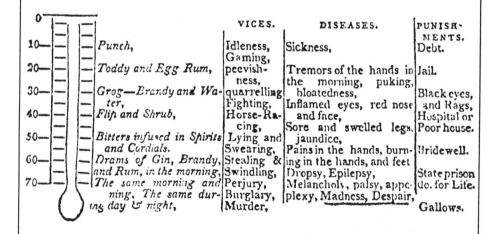

		VICES.	DISEASES.	PUNISH-MENTS.
10 —	Punch,	Idleness, Gaming,	Sickness,	Debt.
20 —	Toddy and Egg Rum,	peevish-ness,	Tremors of the hands in the morning, puking,	Jail.
30 —	Grog—Brandy and Water,	quarrelling Fighting,	bloatedness, Inflamed eyes, red nose	Black eyes, and Rags,
40 —	Flip and Shrub,	Horse-Racing,	and face, Sore and swelled legs,	Hospital or Poor house.
50 —	Bitters infused in Spirits and Cordials.	Lying and Swearing,	jaundice, Pains in the hands, burn-	Bridewell.
60 —	Drams of Gin, Brandy, and Rum, in the morning,	Stealing & Swindling,	ing in the hands, and feet Dropsy, Epilepsy,	State prison
70 —	The same morning and evening. The same during day & night,	Perjury, Burglary, Murder,	Melancholy, palsy, appe-plexy, Madness, Despair,	do. for Life. Gallows.

Figure 2. *Benjamin Rush's* A Moral and Physical Thermometer, *reproduced here from the 8th (1814) edition. Reprinted frequently, this illustration expressed the views of the temperance movement.*

cider plunged to levels so low that by 1849 American adults were drinking 75% less absolute alcohol than they had drunk just two decades before.

Temperance agitation on the legal front reached its peak in the early 1850s with the onset of what has been termed the "first great wave" of statewide prohibition. It began in Maine in 1851 and by 1855 a total of thirteen states had adopted "Maine laws." The intent of these laws was primarily to abolish public intoxication, not private drinking, and thereby to protect the American family from drunken disorder. Many of the laws were repealed soon after they were passed.

Even though the 1850s witnessed the greatest legislative victories for temperance reform, per capita consumption of beer increased from 1.6 gallons in 1850 to 3.8 gallons in 1860. America's switch to beer drinking was led

The American "Temperance Crusade," which continued until the passage of national prohibition legislation in 1919, dramatically changed American drinking customs. Like many other social movements, temperance contained elements of religious revivalism, social reform, concern for public health, and intolerance for alternative viewpoints.

by the hoards of German and middle-European immigrants who brought with them both a taste for malt liquors and the skills necessary for brewing them. Under the German brewmasters, beer and ale came to rank among the nation's favorite beverages.

After the Civil War thousands of prospectors, miners, cardsharks, and soldiers of fortune began to migrate to Colorado, California, and Montana in search of gold. As immigration to the Western territories accelerated, one institution came to epitomize the frontier drinking style: the saloon. Although the saloon was initially modeled after the New England inns and taverns, it quickly adapted to the social needs and drinking styles of the frontier.

The first saloons were typically rudimentary buildings, consisting of little more than a shack with a row of barrels for a bar. Adorned by paintings of naked women or Custer's last stand, the saloon's decor mirrored the unrefined and aggressive characteristics of its patrons.

The saloon proliferated on the western frontier to such an extent that in many towns drinking establishments frequently outnumbered all other businesses. The most important functions of the saloon were to provide entertainment,

THE EMIGRANT'S GUIDE TO THE GOLD MINES.

THREE WEEKS

IN THE

GOLD MINES,

OR

ADVENTURES WITH THE GOLD DIGGERS OF CALIFORNIA

In August, 1848.

TOGETHER WITH

ADVICE TO EMIGRANTS,

WITH FULL INSTRUCTIONS UPON THE BEST METHOD OF GETTING THERE, LIVING, EXPENSES, ETC. ETC. AND A

COMPLETE DESCRIPTION OF THE COUNTRY,

With a Map and Illustrations.

Y HENRY I. SIMPSON,

OF THE NEW YORK VOLUNTEERS.

NEW YORK:

JOYCE AND CO., 40 ANN STREET.

1848.

Guidebooks promoting the prospect of immediate wealth lured thousands of immigrants to California in the middle of the 19th century. As varying ethnic drinking customs were added to the melting pot, new and more explosive drinking styles emerged.

diversion, and, of course, liquid refreshment. In addition to the standard games of billiards, poker, and checkers, the saloon frequently sponsored special activities such as dances, lotteries, contests, and prizefights. These entertainments were designed to attract large crowds and to serve as a focal activity for what the saloonkeeper no doubt hoped would be a night of prolonged drinking.

The convergence of large numbers of ambitious, unmarried, male adventure-seekers on the western frontier created the kind of social disorder long celebrated in legend and Hollywood movies. Barroom brawls, the reckless shooting of guns, and general drunkenness became commonplace. Alcohol-related deaths, often from exposure and ensuing pneumonia, contributed to the harsh reality of frontier life. Cold winters took a steady toll of the malnourished, chronically intoxicated unfortunates who failed to find their fortunes in the West.

The American frontier offered adventure, cheap spirits, and weak law enforcement, but provided few leisure activities other than drinking. Those whose dreams went unfulfilled sought comfort in "rotgut" liquor.

Four factors seem to have been influential in the development of the explosive drinking style that emerged on the western frontier. The first was the ready availability of cheap intoxicants. Because it was relatively easy to transport, whiskey was often the only beverage that could be hauled long distances over rugged terrain. In fact, frontier whiskey often consisted of pure alcohol mixed with water. Its wretched taste was reflected in such names as "extract of scorpions," "San Juan Paralyzer" and "Taos Lightning." By the early 1870s technological improvements, which included bottling and pasteurization, led to the development of regional breweries such as Schlitz, Pabst, Blatz, and Budweiser. Beer soon took its place beside whiskey as a favorite beverage in the West.

A second factor affecting the western drinking style was the character of the people attracted to the frontier. Men who were unemployed, rootless, and alienated were particularly attracted to the West. This, in combination with their itinerant life style, made the men prone to develop drinking problems.

In western mining towns the saloon served a variety of important functions, such as recreation hall, employment center, and meeting place.

The third ingredient was the nature of labor and leisure on the frontier. Work on the trail and in the mines was long and monotonous and drinking served as a relief from the drudgery. Thus, the long periods of work were often broken by brief periods of intense drinking.

A final factor contributing to the development of the western drinking style was the lack of social controls on the frontier. Not only were there no constraints on the marketing and production of alcoholic beverages, but there were not enough peace officers to control lawbreakers. With the enactment of legal controls and the emergence of more stable communities, the western saloon eventually became more respectable, and so did its clientele.

Westward expansion and the growth of the frontier drinking style were aspects of a much larger pattern of social change taking place in the United States. Massive immigration and rapid industrialization dramatically altered working conditions, and family and community life in American cities and towns. The social problems associated with the industrial cities of the East and Midwest seemed even worse than the lawlessness and licentiousness on the frontier. When middle-class Americans sought an explanation for the disorder and disease they observed around them, temperance advocates were only too ready to point out the apparent association between drinking, the saloon, and the problems of society.

Saloons appeared in the growing urban centers, especially in the slum areas where opposition to prohibition legislation among expanding ethnic populations was especially strong. In addition to serving alcohol, the saloon provided a convenient meeting place for groups of workingmen. The backrooms and halls were frequently used by social clubs, labor unions, fraternal lodges, and other organizations. Saloon halls also hosted dances and wedding and christening receptions, especially for immigrant groups. Other attractions included the notorious "free lunch," which was provided only because the law required that food be served in drinking establishments.

In the midst of the population expansion in the late 19th century, the drinking patterns of the new immigrants came under special scrutiny by the native-born Americans who had achieved middle-class status. In Boston and New

York the Irish consistently were foremost among all nationalities in their reputation for drunkenness and disorderly conduct, though the Scots and English were not far behind. Why were the Irish, English, and Scottish immigrants more likely to develop drinking problems? Whereas large numbers of Italian, German, and Jewish immigrants were also regular drinkers, their alcohol problems did not seem as bad. A likely explanation seems to be the common patterns of drinking that developed in England, Ireland, and Scotland during the late 18th century and early 19th century. Each of these countries had developed strongly ingrained drinking customs related to the social use of alcohol at work, marriage ceremonies, funerals, baptisms, and during business transactions.

After immigration to America, heavy drinking grew even further in significance, taking on a separate identity and cultural meaning. The Irish ranked lowest among all ethnic

European immigrants arriving in the United States in the 1890s not only brought new drinking customs, but also brought a variety of alcohol-related problems. Poverty, discrimination, and the need for a place to socialize often led them to the saloon and a career of drinking.

groups in the proportion of intact families among its emigrants. Thus, the bachelor drinking group was often a primary social unit of the young Irish-American male. Hard drinking with the boys not only became a way of demonstrating one's Irishness, but also provided a sense of ethnic identification.

Despite the progressive increase in per capita beer consumption during the latter part of the 19th century, drinking in America had become as erratic as its restless and heterogeneous population. Both drinking and abstinence became closely identified with a specific social class, religion, and ethnic group. For example, middle- and upper-class Protestants generally saw total abstinence as a symbol of respectability and as a means to achieve health, success, and happiness. Books on popular manners and advice consistently associated temperance with such virtues as industry and thrift.

By the 1880s the temperance movement had helped to establish various stereotypes: total abstinence from alcohol with middle-class respectability; beer drinking with being German; whiskey drinking with being Irish; and wine drinking with being Italian. These associations were used as a basis of racial, class, and religious discrimination, which separated the "unwashed" immigrants from the "native" Americans.

The March to Prohibition

Amidst growing concern over urbanization, immigration, and the social disorder prevalent in almost every section of the country, alcoholic beverages and the urban saloon were singled out and given particular attention. Led by the Women's Christian Temperance Union and the Prohibition party, a second wave of prohibition legislation was enacted throughout the country in the 1880s and early 1890s. Five states adopted constitutional prohibition, while 15 states passed local option laws that allowed the voters in each town or city to vote for (wet) or against (dry) the sale of alcoholic beverages in their communities.

As the second great wave of prohibition sentiment began to fade during the "Gay Nineties," a new organization emerged—the Antisaloon League of America. Their ultimate goal was to dry up the country bit by bit through local option laws and statewide prohibition. In 1913 the league declared itself in favor of national prohibition by amendment to the federal constitution.

By 1916 the issue of U.S. involvement in World War I threatened to overwhelm the debate over prohibition. But

Organizations such as the Women's Christian Temperance Union (WCTU) led a powerful campaign to convince Americans that alcohol was a poison that should be legally banned. The WCTU succeeded in imposing their own variety of alcohol education on almost every school system in the nation. By the time prohibition went into effect in 1919, practically every American adult had heard that "Alcohol means Poison."

as President Woodrow Wilson prepared to ask Congress for a declaration of war, the prohibition forces seized the moment and, under the guise of food conservation, tied a dry legislation amendment to the president's war program. The amendment passed easily in both the House and the Senate, and progressed through the states in record time to become law on January 16, 1919.

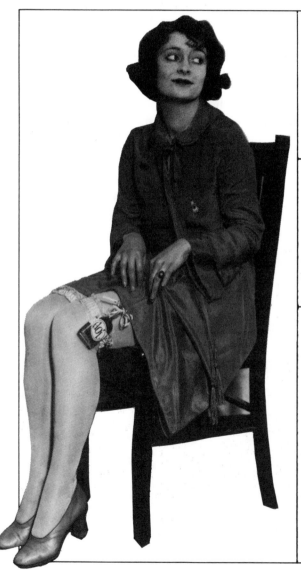

Just as "head shops" today openly sell drug paraphernalia, in the 1920s, during Prohibition, enterprising salesmen marketed drinking-related products. To conceal a few ounces of bathtub gin from federal agents, one could buy garter flasks and hollow books and high heel shoes.

Prohibition initially enjoyed wide popular support, but it also created a host of problems. Enforcement was difficult and could only be carried out sporadically. Home production of wine and beer was widespread. Alcohol could also still be purchased legally for "medicinal" purposes after obtaining a doctor's prescription. During the 1920s illegal smuggling, supported by a growing network of organized crime, grew into a major business enterprise. When consumed in large quantities, these bootleg liquors sometimes resulted in paralysis, blindness, or even death. With the increasing supply of both domestic and imported alcohol, thousands of private drinking clubs, or "speakeasies," were opened in the major cities. These catered especially to business and professional people, who could afford the exorbitant prices charged for good liquor.

Although Prohibition succeeded in abolishing the saloon, reducing per capita alcohol consumption, and decreas-

Speakeasies, illegal saloons of the Prohibition era, gained their name because patrons had to identify themselves quietly before gaining entry. Thousands existed under the guise of private clubs and restaurants.

ing the number of alcohol-related problems seen in public, it also introduced a new generation of young, upwardly mobile, middle-class Americans to the drinking of illegal hard liquor. Just as drug use became fashionable during the 1960s among the avant-garde and middle-class youth, unlawful drinking became emblematic of the "Roaring Twenties."

Changing public attitudes and the need for tax revenues to combat the Great Depression led to the repeal of Prohibition under the Roosevelt administration in 1933. Except for taxation, all authority to control the manufacture and sale of alcoholic beverages was turned over to the states. Some states adopted the monopoly, or control, system by which wholesale and retail operations were largely controlled by state governments. The remaining states regulated availability by the license system, which gave each state the power to grant manufacturers, wholesalers, and retailers the privilege of conducting business. In both systems, the regulations were designed to prevent the abuses of the saloon, promote public safety and welfare, and protect the health of citizens. Under the new control system, the economic depression and high prices kept per capita consumption well below pre-Prohibition levels until after World War II.

Contemporary American Drinking Customs

Since the 1950s American drinking patterns have taken on a new dimension, fluctuating and varying according to a variety of social and economic factors. American drinking today is a patchwork of traditional and modern customs, related as much to the age and sex of the drinker as to religious, ethnic, and economic backgrounds. Per capita consumption has risen steadily, with beer accounting for slightly more than half of the total alcohol consumed.

Surveys indicate that about a third of the total population abstains from alcohol, another third drinks only occasionally, and that the remaining third accounts for most of the alcohol consumed. More men than women drink, and men drink more heavily than women. Alcohol use by youth has risen since the 1950s, with more than 90% of high school seniors using alcohol within a given year. About 6% of the seniors surveyed in 1981 drank daily or nearly daily,

Table 1

STATE	SPIRITS	WINE	BEER	ABSOLUTE ALCOHOL	RANK
Apparent Consumption of Alcoholic Beverages and Total Absolute Alcohol*					
Alabama	2.12	0.91	21.87	2.03	44
Alaska	4.16	3.53	31.63	3.73	3
Arizona	2.78	3.00	39.52	3.41	9
Arkansas	1.76	0.87	21.48	1.85	49
California	3.22	5.29	31.49	3.57	5
Colorado	3.51	3.66	33.41	3.54	6
Connecticut	2.92	2.93	24.01	2.76	27
Delaware	3.32	1.93	29.67	3.04	17
Florida	3.47	2.65	33.85	3.40	10
Georgia	2.80	1.43	25.33	2.55	33
Hawaii	3.18	3.61	30.95	3.28	11
Idaho	2.02	2.15	33.62	2.69	30
Illinois	2.86	2.42	30.62	2.96	19
Indiana	1.88	1.21	26.70	2.18	42
Iowa	1.80	0.82	31.33	2.30	38
Kansas	1.60	0.89	25.33	1.96	46
Kentucky	1.90	0.71	22.15	1.92	47
Louisiana	2.60	1.97	29.96	2.75	28
Maine	2.64	2.08	29.01	2.74	29
Maryland	3.34	2.39	30.41	3.15	14
Massachusetts	3.04	3.12	30.84	3.15	15
Michigan	2.56	2.12	31.75	2.84	22
Minnesota	2.82	1.75	29.15	2.78	26
Mississippi	2.23	0.81	25.88	2.24	40
Missouri	1.94	1.52	29.24	2.37	37
Montana	2.66	1.57	40.61	3.20	12
Nebraska	2.18	1.38	33.33	2.64	32
Nevada	8.97	6.62	49.68	7.05	1
New Hampshire	7.14	4.19	44.06	5.66	2
New Jersey	2.68	3.22	25.90	2.79	25
New Mexico	2.38	2.49	36.58	3.03	18
New York	2.81	3.25	26.21	2.86	21
North Carolina	2.09	1.63	24.21	2.22	41
North Dakota	2.79	1.25	31.29	2.79	24
Ohio	1.78	1.55	28.81	2.28	39
Oklahoma	2.02	1.07	24.00	2.10	43
Oregon	2.38	3.68	29.89	2.90	20
Pennsylvania	1.80	1.64	30.33	2.38	36
Rhode Island	2.81	3.83	31.26	3.17	13
South Carolina	2.91	1.34	27.34	2.68	31
South Dakota	2.56	1.33	26.58	2.49	34
Tennessee	1.75	0.83	25.61	2.02	45
Texas	2.06	1.55	37.99	2.82	23
Utah	1.50	1.07	21.59	1.77	50
Vermont	3.86	3.63	33.62	3.70	4
Virginia	2.21	1.64	27.18	2.41	35
Washington	2.77	3.73	30.96	3.12	16
West Virginia	1.91	0.69	21.42	1.89	48
Wisconsin	3.06	2.15	39.96	3.42	8
Wyoming	3.32	1.73	40.59	3.51	7
District of Columbia	7.51	7.32	31.74	5.72	
U.S.A.	2.60	2.51	29.78	2.82	

*In U.S. gallons per capita of the population aged 14+, by state, in 1978.

and 41% drank enough (five or more drinks per occasion) to become intoxicated twice a month. Heavy drinking among males reaches its peak at about age 30, while females tend to drink most heavily after age 40.

Substantial variation exists across states in the type and amounts of alcohol consumed. States with the highest per capita consumption among adults are Nevada, New Hampshire, Alaska, Wisconsin, and Wyoming. States with the lowest drinking rates are Utah, Alabama, Arkansas, West Virginia, and Kentucky. These regional variations reflect such factors as tourism (Nevada, New Hampshire), the frontier-drinking style (Alaska, Wyoming), the brewing industry (Wisconsin), and religious proscriptions (Utah and the Southern states).

One study of the major white American ethnic groups found that the Irish are the most likely to be drinkers (only 8% were abstainers) and are more likely to consume three

This "strikers special" appeared in the window of a Chicago tavern just as 90,000 steelworkers prepared to go on strike. Drink discounts such as this can provide an incentive to drink heavily.

or more drinks of hard liquor at a sitting. Although there were also low rates of total abstention among Jews and Italians, these groups were found to drink less per occasion and to experience fewer drinking problems. Among other American ethnic groups, Hispanics tend to have greater proportions of heavier drinkers, while blacks tend to drink less.

The drinking habits of the American Indians are the most misunderstood and difficult to fathom. Contrary to the "firewater myth" that all Indians are biologically predisposed to drink excessively, anthropological studies have shown that many tribes drink in moderation or not at all. Among certain Arctic Coast and Northwest Coast Indian tribes, alcoholism is thought to be rare or nonexistent, despite occasional drunkenness. Other tribes, such as the

Members of the Los Angeles Indian Lodge discuss problems of alcoholism. It is estimated that one-third of the nation's Native Americans have drinking difficulties. In the atmosphere of the Lodge, alcoholics dry out, attend Alcoholics Anonymous meetings, and face their problems.

Hopis, rarely get drunk in public, though they drink regularly and have high rates of alcoholic cirrhosis of the liver. Still other tribes, such as the Apaches, drink more in public settings and tend to experience problems associated with intoxication, such as aggressiveness and a proneness to accidents.

American drinking customs are concentrated around three types of social settings: the home, the cocktail party, and the public drinking establishment. The place where most Americans drink most often is the home. Here ethnic drinking customs are likely to prevail, especially with respect to mealtime drinking by Italians or ceremonial drinking by Jews. Private parties are the occasions where Americans tend to drink most heavily, although the amount of drinking depends upon the age and socioeconomic level of the drink-

Despite the continuing presence of skid row derelicts, the actual numbers of chronic alcoholics declined dramatically in the 1920s and 1930s. During the Prohibition era, alcohol was expensive and difficult to obtain outside of the major cities. After the repeal of Prohibition in 1933, which coincided with the Great Depression, many Americans were too poor to drink regularly.

ers. The highest level of drinking occurs among teenagers and college students at "keggers," or beer parties, where large groups and loud music are the rule. More sedate are the wine and cheese gatherings and cocktail parties typically organized by married couples.

Americans tend to drink heavily at bars and taverns, whose decor and character are closely related to the clientele. Singles bars cater to unmarried males and females under age 30, providing a forum for dancing and courting. Cocktail lounges appeal to an older and more affluent clientele, while neighborhood bars are frequented most by working-class men and members of ethnic minorities. Skid-

The clientele of America's working-class bars sport a variety of headgear, from cowboy hats to hard hats. Neighborhood taverns and country-and-western bars cater to workingmen by creating a masculine ambience.

row bars are typically located in the inner-city slums where urban alcoholics drink. Country and western bars are more often located in rural settings. The ambience of these bars has been described by popular singers such as George Jones and Merle Haggard in songs like "Back to the Barroom," "What made Milwaukee Famous (beer) Made a Loser out of Me," "Still Doin' Time (in a Honky-tonk Prison)," and "If Drinking Don't Kill Me, Her Memory Will." In recent years many drinking establishments have attempted to entice patrons in the afternoon or early evening hours by drink discounts collectively known as "happy hours." Typical inducements include "twofers" (two drinks for the price of one), nickel beers, and free drinks for women.

Clearly there is no single drinking style or set of drinking customs in the United States that applies broadly to all Americans. Rather, there are a variety of drinking subcultures that influence drinking patterns and problems. Because some of these drinking patterns are learned in the family setting, they are likely to persist from one generation to another.

As ethnic and religious influences become less important to new generations of drinkers, the role of fads, peer groups, and advertising takes on added importance. It is not yet clear what accounts for changing trends in alcohol consumption or drinking customs. During the 1970s wine and cheese parties became popular drinking contexts for the upwardly mobile middle class, perhaps because it gives the party-goers a chance to identify with French *haute cuisine*. During the 1980s "happy hours" became an inducement for singles and business people to drink in the afternoon, and for many youths alcohol became an all too frequent chaser for drugs.

Realizing that in the United States two-thirds of all beer is consumed between 4:00 p.m. and 8:00 p.m., advertisers designated this period "Miller Time" in an effort to capture the group that marketing specialists called "belongers"— workingmen looking for a reprieve after work from the harsh demands of their blue-collar jobs. Given the long and often contentious history of alcohol use in America, it is practically impossible to predict how future drinking customs will evolve, except to say that they are likely to be as dynamic and heterogeneous as America itself.

Falstaff carousing at the Boarshead Tavern in Shakespeare's play Henry IV. *This image epitomizes the Elizabethan public house, where many of the English-speaking world's drinking customs originated.*

CHAPTER 3

DRINKING
AROUND THE WORLD

*T*he European continent is occupied by 13% of the world's population, yet its inhabitants consume about half of the world's alcohol. Because of the great diversity in cultural groups, geography, and historical development, Europe provides a fascinating panorama of drinking customs and rituals. It is also the place where many of the world's drinking customs originated.

Because of its unique climate and geography, Europe is ideally suited to the production of a variety of alcoholic beverages. It is therefore not surprising that different European countries, depending on their specific environments, specialize in the production of wine, beer, and spirits, and that their inhabitants develop specialized beverage preferences in response to local supply. Three relatively distinct areas can be identified according to the production and consumption of alcohol. Firstly, southern Europe, because of its moderate climate and abundance of sunny days, is made up mainly of wine-drinking countries: Portugal, Spain, France, Italy, Switzerland, and Greece. Beer-drinking lands such as Austria, Germany, Czechoslovakia, Denmark, Belgium, Ireland, and Great Britain, abundant in hops and barley, are primarily located in the central areas of Europe. Lastly, the northern countries, Finland, Russia, Norway, Poland, and Sweden, rich in grains and fruits, are partial to the use of spirits.

Spirits-Drinking Countries

What distinguishes people from the Scandinavian countries of Sweden, Norway, Finland, and Iceland is their distinct preference for distilled liquor, their strict government control of the production and sale of alcohol, and their long and still-active temperance tradition. Like the United States, each of these countries briefly experimented with prohibition following World War I. However, American-style bars or taverns are not common in Scandinavia; therefore most drinking takes place in the home or in restaurants, and begins with the familiar word *Skal*, an invocation to drink to health.

Sweden Approximately 50% of the alcohol consumed in Sweden is in the form of spirits. The traditional drink has long been *aquavit*, which is drunk in large quantities on weekends, holidays, and the midsummer festivals. Drinking is restricted almost exclusively to men and is done primarily in the home. Until recently, it was common to drink beer

During malt whiskey's 4- to 12-year aging process, a "leak hunter," such as this one in Scotland, periodically taps the barrels and listens for the hollow sound that marks an excessive loss of spirits.

and aquavit with meals, especially at dinner parties or in restaurants. Since the end of World War II, however, the Swedes have adapted to international customs. As a result, wine has become popular at meals, and beer has become the beverage of choice mainly among young people. As part of this trend, the use of alcohol has increased among women and teenagers.

Until the early 1900s aquavit drinking was widespread. However, the emergence of a strong temperance movement resulted in the suppression of home production and the

In Sweden and Poland small farmers distill and age their surplus fruit to produce a tasty, potent plum brandy, such as the one being sampled above. In Sweden it is called aquavit; *in Poland,* slivovitz.

institution of the so-called Gothenberg system. Under this system, all sales of aquavit are controlled by local municipalities through special nonprofit companies. Further restrictions were imposed on drinking through the Bratt rationing system, which set limits on individual purchases of spirits according to age, sex, occupation, income, and family circumstances. Established during World War I, it was abolished in 1955.

Finland Although the Finns traditionally have had a low level of alcohol consumption, a large proportion of their drinking involves a conscious decision to get drunk. Most drinking is concentrated during weekends, celebrations, and special occasions, and they generally do not drink during meals. Some of the consequences of the Finnish drinking style are a high prevalence of public intoxication, arrests because of drunkenness, and crimes of violence associated with drinking. As in other Scandinavian countries, the national government controls the production and sale of alcohol.

Poland The Poles are among the heaviest liquor drinkers in the world. Yet, drinking is not considered a normal part of everyday life in Poland. Alcohol is not generally consumed with meals, although a vodka before dinner is common, especially among the upper classes. For most of the population, however, vodka is used socially on special occasions, primarily by adult males. Tradition dictates that vodka is a man's drink, and beer is the introductory beverage for

Members of Solidarity, Poland's independent trade union, raise a flag during a clash with government troops in 1982. To maintain order and to raise money for workers, Solidarity leaders enforced strict controls on workers' drinking. This led to a more moderate drinking behavior and a decline in alcohol-related problems.

young people and a permissible substitute for women.

Most drinking in Poland occurs either at home or at the local *chaupa*, similar to an American bar. They are frequently visited in connection with daily activities such as business meetings, trips to the farmer's market, or after work. On weekends men often stop for a drink after church. Another place to drink is the state-owned *restauracja*, where men and women often relax or take care of business over a shot glass of vodka chased by a beer. The most frequent toast is *nazdrowie*, "to your health." The glass is typically emptied in a single gulp, after which it is turned upside down and shaken to indicate that the last drop has been finished.

It is considered impolite to refuse a drink when a toast is offered, which is one of many customs that makes drinking to intoxication the rule rather than the exception among Poles. While drunkenness is considered acceptable for males, public drinking by females is frowned upon. Habitual intoxication is considered reprehensible and is treated harshly.

When drinking takes place at home, it is most likely to occur on Sundays, religious holidays, or special family holidays such as name days, the equivalent of our birthdays. On such occasions the table is spread with ham, fresh vegetables, bread, and the inevitable bottle of vodka or local *slivovitz* (brandy). Another occasion for heavy drinking is weddings, which are not considered successful unless there is an unlimited supply of vodka.

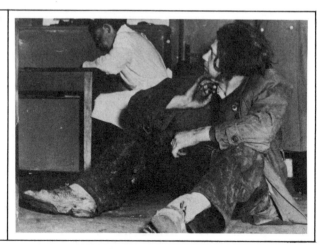

Although strong societal approval is given to regular drinking in European countries, public drunkenness is often treated harshly by the criminal justice system. One alternative, tried by countries such as Poland and Finland, is the use of "sobering-up stations," which deal humanely with drunks, such as this one in Warsaw.

In Poland during the 1960s and 1970s a dramatic increase in alcohol consumption paralleled the general rise in standard of living. With the emergence of the free trade union movement (Solidarity), however, moderate drinking or abstinence was enforced among the workers in order to maintain discipline and to serve as a symbol of their determination to reform the government.

Wine-Drinking Countries

In the wine-producing Mediterranean countries of Spain, Portugal, Italy, France, and Greece wine is a standard dietary beverage. Its use as a social lubricant, medicine, and stimulant is supported by popular attitudes and cultural traditions dating back to Roman times. Although drunkenness is not common, these countries have high levels of consumption and lead the world in mortality from cirrhosis of the liver, a disease caused primarily by excessive drinking.

In France and Italy, where wine is considered a healthful drink, custom prescribes the use of certain wines during illness and recovery. This late 19th-century ad for Mariani wine, which contained cocaine, portrays the beverage as a panacea for all ills and even bears the pope's approval.

Drinking tends to be integrated into daily activities and rituals, more for its social and dietary value than for its psychological effects. Children are introduced to alcohol gradually and naturally, and there are few legal restrictions on the availability of alcoholic beverages.

France In every walk of life, in every social class, and from the cradle to the grave, alcohol plays a prominent role in the daily life of the French. Just about any occasion or event, be it social, religious, or political, is an appropriate occasion to drink. In lower Normandy it is customary to offer a friend a cup of coffee "watered down" with a copious helping of apple brandy (*café Calvados*). At work, blue-collar employees and agricultural laborers often drink wine or beer during their breaks, and continue drinking wine with their noonday meal. After work it is not unusual for the men to pass a few hours in the local café before returning home to the evening meal, which is again accompanied by a bottle of

Harvesting grapes in France is difficult but rewarding work that typically involves the whole family. Women and children clip bunches of grapes from the vines and empty them into the porter's bucket, in which they are taken to the chateau or local wine cooperative for pressing and fermentation.

wine. Mailmen, salesmen, truck drivers, and other itinerant workers typically spend a large portion of their day drinking in cafés and restaurants as they make their daily rounds.

The use of alcohol to complement food has been developed to a fine art by the French. Indeed, the words connoisseur, savoir faire, and savoir-vivre, all connoting an appreciation for good living, are closely connected with the art of matching food and wine most harmoniously. To do this properly, one must follow a prescribed ritual, which dictates the appropriate alcoholic beverage to accompany each part of the meal. To open the meal and stimulate the appetite, one first takes an apéritif such as vermouth, Pernod, or anise. During the meal one chooses a red, white, or rosé dinner wine to complement the main course. Another wine may be called for when the cheese arrives, and champagne or sparkling burgundy may be ordered as a dessert wine. Following the meal, a "digestif" of liqueur or brandy is usually taken to facilitate digestion.

A repair shop at the French wine market is available to take care of damaged barrels. Here, expert cask makers still employ the old methods taught at a coopers' school within the **Halle aux Vins.**

Although the term "alcoholic Republic" was first used to describe American drinking patterns following the American Revolutionary War, the term applies equally well to contemporary France. Of all the nations of the world, France has undisputed leadership in practically all things alcoholic. Not only do the French drink more per capita, they also lead the world in the production of alcohol and alcoholics.

Since the Middle Ages wine has been the national beverage and one of the major agricultural products of France. Although a significant proportion of France's fine bordeaux, burgundies, and champagnes are exported to all parts of the world, the less expensive wines are consumed domestically. In fact, there is hardly a province in France without its local brandy or wine. In Normandy, hard cider and Calvados, a brandy distilled from cider, are the traditional beverages. In Bordeaux, cognac and armagnac are distilled from the local

An Italian barrel maker works on a large wine cask, climbing inside to smooth the wooden staves. Constructed just outside Rome, the casks will later be filled with wine from the famed town of Frascati.

wines. In Alsace, close to the German border, a kirsch brandy is made from cherries. Large amounts of beer are produced as well.

The importance of alcohol in the French economy is reflected in what is perhaps the most elaborate network of popular attitudes, social customs, religious rituals, and historical traditions ever developed by a large cultural group. The tremendous production of alcoholic beverages in France accounts for a considerable portion of France's domestic economy and foreign trade. Approximately 10% of the population is involved in some way with the alcoholic beverage industry.

For many of the French daily life revolves around the café, a neighborhood institution that serves a variety of social, psychological, and political functions. Like the English pub and the American bar, the French café is often a home away from home. Its predominantly male clientele constitutes a cross section of French society. Early in the morning delivery men and farmers stop for a *petit rouge* on their way to market, followed by mailmen, policemen, and truck drivers ordering the same or perhaps a midmorning

French workers read about the death of a president at a typical Parisian bistro. Once called the "Parlements of the People" because of their role in political organizing, the French cafés serve a variety of functions. On somber occasions such as this one, the café becomes a place for sharing information, opinions, and feelings. In happier times, it is a place where the popular toast, à votre santé, is offered.

café Calva or a beer. After the businessmen's lunch has been washed down with a carafe of local wine, the café in the afternoon may be dominated by the factory workers, who drink until supper time.

In the evening the clientele of the café is typically young people and regular patrons who gather to talk, play cards, or watch television. Although public drunkenness is not as prevalent in France as it is in the Scandinavian countries, the regularity of café drinking contributes to the custom of *la tournee*, which requires that each person buy a round of drinks. The custom of treating extends to just about any occasion that will serve as an excuse for drinking.

In addition to the everyday customs of drinking with meals at home and between meals at the café, practically every occasion in French life provides a reason for drinking. At engagements, weddings, baptisms, and funerals wine and spirits are consumed freely. Religious holidays and festivals, such as the Carnival at Nice, have traditionally been times of heavy drinking. Among the grape growers and other agricultural workers, ceremonial drinking occurs at the time of the planting and the harvest.

This parade in Nice, France, ushers in the Carnival celebrations that sweep through the Catholic countries of Europe and Latin America in the weeks before Lent. This is a time when copious drinking of alcoholic beverages—behavior originating in Roman festivals—meets with little social disapproval.

The pervasive use of alcohol in French society is a logical outgrowth of longtime attitudes that have glorified drinking and trivialized its negative aspects. Celebrated in song, poetry, and popular sayings, wine and spirits are associated with health, strength, virility, courage, friendship, romance, and happiness. Rooted more in superstition and self-delusion than fact, these beliefs confer upon alcohol magical powers to destroy germs, improve circulation, reduce fever, cure colds, and nourish the body. Thousands of documented folk remedies for health problems, ranging from colds to cancer, prescribe the use of wine or spirits. With the support of more than 35 Roman Catholic patron saints, the French have imbued alcoholic beverages with an aura reserved by most cultures for religious objects.

Greece Drinking patterns in contemporary Greece can be traced to their historical roots in classical antiquity. With the exception of a few ritualized social occasions during which drunkenness is permissible for men, drinking of wine

This engraving by Jacques Lagniet, in which a dishonest wine seller dilutes his wine with water as his wife and a baker kiss behind his back, makes light of an old French proverb: "He is quite wise, he puts water in his wine." Several other French proverbs are quoted in this picture: "Where the hostess is pretty the wine is good." "A pretty hostess is hard on the pocketbook." "Cloudy wine won't break your teeth."

in the home is still done in moderation. Here alcoholic beverages, especially *retsina*, a white or rosé table wine, are typically consumed with meals. Alcohol consumption is also a normal part of Greek hospitality. Guests and visitors are offered sweets along with small glasses of spirits. In rural areas, the beverages served, such as *raki*, a brandy, and *ouzo*, an anise-flavored liqueur, are locally made or home-brewed products. As in Italy and Spain, wine is often mixed with water.

In public settings drinking most frequently takes place in coffee houses, *tavernas* (informal restaurants), or *bouzoukia* (nightclubs where popular singers are accompanied by musicians playing the bouzouki and other instruments). Although in Greece alcohol is consumed in moderation in the home, in certain places and at certain times excess is permitted. One such occasion is the celebration of *Apokreas* (carnival), which occurs just before the onset of Lent. Throughout Greece and most of the Catholic countries of

To open the Fiesta de la Vendimia (Harvest Festival) in Jerez de la Frontera, Spain, the queen carries grapes which will be blessed by a priest and then symbolically stomped in a wooden trough.

Europe people celebrate with revelry reminiscent of the ancient Greek and Roman festivals. At such times excessive drinking is encouraged, while violence and licentiousness are tolerated to an extent not otherwise accepted.

At restaurants or taverns drunkenness is sometimes observed among the very rich. According to a prescribed ritual (which also requires the drinker to assume the costs of his excess), smashing crockery, destroying furniture, and pouring liquor on the floor are tolerated in public places as symbols of the drinker's disdain for material goods.

Alcoholic drinks are important in the sealing of bargains or contracts, symbolic of the mystical potency that gives alcohol a special role in many social rituals. As portrayed in *Zorba the Greek*, when a business agreement is reached, a drink is typically ordered by both parties so that the agreement "holds good."

Actor Anthony Quinn celebrates the opening of his movie, Zorba the Greek, *by performing a dance native to Greece. As one of the oldest wine-producing societies, Greece has a rich tradition of drinking customs and rituals, including singing and dancing in taverns and restaurants.*

Alcohol has gained similar meanings in association with religious rituals. Wine plays a major symbolic role in various ceremonies of the Greek Orthodox Church. Not only is it consumed in the communion service, but wine is a part of certain ceremonies and every religious festival. For example, the festival of St. Trypon, patron saint of vines and wine, is devoted exclusively to the celebration of the fruits of the vine.

Beer-Drinking Countries

In West Germany, East Germany, Austria, Czechoslovakia, Denmark, Belgium, Great Britain, and Ireland beer is the alcoholic beverage of preference. Before the 19th century, beer was made different from ale by the addition of hops. It

The October grape harvest in a 1702 engraving by Karl Gustav Amling. Here men stamp on the grapes with their bare feet, which break the skins without cracking the bitter seeds, allowing the juice to escape. A mechanical press with a screw top is also being used to extract the residue from the broken grapes.

was a town drink in contrast to the unhopped (and therefore unstable) ale, which was brewed in the countryside. With the industrialization of brewing in the 18th century, all malt liquor, such as beer and ale, became hopped. The term "beer" became associated with the popular porter and stout, while "ale" came to mean the pale, clear beverage that did not have to be aged. Like wine and spirits, beer has become associated with a variety of drinking customs and rituals that play a unique role in the national identities of a number of countries.

Germany Germany has always been classified as a beer-drinking land. Today, West Germany is not only one of the world's largest consumers of beer, but also ranks seventh in total alcohol consumption in the world. Beer drinking is equally divided between the home and public drinking places, such as beer halls, taverns, and restaurants. Although alcoholism and drunkenness are major problems in Germany, drinking to intoxication is less the goal of drinking than the consequence of the sociability that accompanies it. Unlike the Scandinavian countries, German attitudes toward the use of alcohol are extremely liberal.

The most popular place to enjoy German beer is at one of the ubiquitous beer halls, which are typically the largest

An outdoor **Biergarten,** *typically attached to taverns, restaurants, and beer halls, is a popular place to pass a summer afternoon in Germany and Austria.*

meeting places of cities and towns. Beer halls are actually converted breweries, which explains why some are large enough to accommodate as many as 5,000 drinkers.

The most celebrated beer-drinking city is Munich. So important is beer to the citizens of Munich that there are special festivals, such as Bock Beer Time and Strong Beer Time, that exist solely to promote the drinking of special brews. The biggest of the festivals is *Fasching*, a national New Year's carnival designed to enliven the dreary months of January and February. During these months in Munich it is customary to attend masquerade balls, which place a premium on exotic dress, bizarre behavior, and beer.

Munich also organizes the greatest beer festival in the world, the annual Oktoberfest. First begun in 1810 on the occasion of the marriage of Crown Prince Ludwig, Oktoberfest consists of two weeks of carousing, overeating, singing, dancing, and, of course, continuous beer drinking.

Austria Although Austria is also considered a beer-drinking country, large amounts of wine and spirits are consumed as

An Austrian wine lover admires a bottle he just purchased for 80 cents at this "wine automat." Innkeepers are opposed to these machines, which they claim provide juveniles with an easy way to obtain alcoholic beverages.

well. A significant proportion of the adult population drinks regularly, and a variety of settings are provided for this purpose. In rural settings the *Gasthaus* is a place where local men meet to play cards, discuss matters of mutual interest, and drink substantial quantities of beer. In urban settings, beer drinking takes place in the bistros, cafés, and German-style beer halls.

Between these rural and urban drinking contexts is found a unique Austrian institution, the wine garden. Located in vineyard gardens on the outskirts of the city, these outdoor drinking places are known as *Buschenschranken* because of the "bush" of evergreen boughs traditionally hung to announce that the vineyard is open for business. What distinguishes the wine gardens from beer halls and cafés is their emphasis on moderation, the involvement of entire families, and the romantic atmosphere created by the rural setting. Occasionally, musicians play among the tables. The clientele is middle class and quite varied: older male

Local custom dictates the kinds of food that accompany drinking. Beer and pretzels are to the Germans what wine and cheese are to the French. One reason why public intoxication is a persistent problem in Germany is suggested by the size of the typical beer stein shown in this picture.

"regulars," groups of single women, and family groups consisting of parents, grandparents, and children. Wine gardens are popular during summer and autumn, especially among Sunday afternoon strollers returning from a hike in the countryside. In early September they are often the center of wine-tasting festivals when the new vintage is introduced.

Belgium Located between wine-drinking France and beer-drinking Holland, Belgium has no truly national beverage. At the end of the 19th century excessive aquavit drinking among industrial workers led to restrictions on the drinking of spirits in public establishments. Since that time Belgium has become a predominantly beer-drinking country, although the French-speaking Walloons favor wine. Liquor is consumed primarily in the home, while most social drinking takes place at bars and cafés.

Great Britain Drinking is closely associated with the public houses (pubs) in Great Britain. These neighborhood taverns have traditionally served as social centers and as places to conduct business or union activities. The pub, for

A bemedaled English pikeman enjoys a pint of ale during a break in the annual Lord Mayor's Pageant. In medieval times an ale knight was a person noted more for his exploits in the public house than on the fields of battle. Today many of the drinking customs originating in Shakespearean times are continued by ale-drinking Englishmen in London's pubs.

the most part, is a male enclave, a place to go after work for a pint of ale and a game of darts. Because of legal regulations, pubs must interrupt their service for at least two hours in the afternoon and must close at 10:30 p.m. These regulations were designed to prevent excessive drinking from interfering with family life and the efficiency of the country's labor force.

Ireland Despite their reputation for love of whiskey, the Irish are mainly beer drinkers. This has been true since the 19th century when a strong temperance movement, led by the famous Father Mathew, successfully changed Ireland's drinking habits.

Unlike their Irish-American cousins, the European Irish have a high proportion of total abstainers, especially among women; have a relatively low level of average alcohol consumption; and experience fewer alcohol-related problems than most nationalities.

Like the English, the Irish drink mostly in pubs. Little drinking is done at home or with meals, and drinking tends to be concentrated into weekend periods, or during festivals and vacations.

Three young men on their way to a pub pass one of Scotland's ubiquitous beer advertisements. Contrary to popular opinion, drinking customs that encourage heavy beer consumption are as hazardous to health and safety as those that encourage liquor drinking.

Summary

Since the 1960s a number of trends have taken place in Europe that have begun to change some of the traditional European drinking practices. One change has been a shift from what were once clear-cut national preferences. For example, the French are drinking more beer and less wine. Spirits-drinking countries are drinking more American-style distilled beverages. And total per capita consumption has risen in almost all countries, except France. Drinking practices are thus becoming more similar among the European communities.

These changes are related, to some extent, to the adoption of less stereotyped, more international drinking customs by the young. Women are also more likely to prefer new types of light or mixed drinks rather than the traditional beverages associated with male drinking. In addition, the growth of tourism and the large number of foreign workers in the European countries have exposed large segments of foreign populations to the drinking customs of other cultures. Given these trends, it is likely that Europe will maintain its leadership in practically all alcohol consumption and production areas for many years.

Animals can learn to drink alcoholic beverages, but complex drinking customs are uniquely human. While the sight of a beer-drinking dog may be amusing to inebriated bar patrons, animals have a low tolerance to alcohol and can even die from drinking too much.

The Chinese philosopher Confucius warned his followers almost 2,500 years ago against drinking excessively at religious ceremonies. Religious doctrines have often determined the appropriate uses of alcohol.

CHAPTER 4

DRINKING IN
LATIN AMERICA, AFRICA, ASIA

*T*hough drinking is not regularly associated with Africa, Asia, and many Third-World nations, the use of alcoholic beverages in these parts of the world often predates by centuries European colonization. In fact, as early as 478 B.C.E. Confucious warned his Chinese compatriots against the vice of drunkenness commonly observed at religious rites.

Latin America

Alcohol use was an established part of the Indian cultures of Central and South America well before the arrival of the Spanish conquerors in the 16th century. As with the ancient Mediterranean civilizations, drinking was an important element of various communal occasions, such as harvest festivals, weddings, burials, and religious celebrations. In South America the main alcoholic drink was *chicha*, a type of wine fermented from ingredients such as apples, strawberries, yucca, oats, and corn. In some parts of the Andes, the brewing of a new batch is signaled to neighbors by displaying a cross on the roof. Sacred to the Mayan civilization of Central America was a beverage called *balche*. Fermented from a combination of honey and tree bark, *balche* is still prepared today by the people of the Mexican Yucatan. In

Mexico, the Aztecs drank a beverage called *pulque*, which was made from the juice of the agave cactus. Both *chicha* and *pulque* had relatively low amounts of alcohol.

Like the Egyptians, Greeks, and Romans, the Aztecs considered their *pulque* a gift from the gods. Although drunkenness was forbidden on most occasions, worshipers at major religious celebrations and holy days were expected to get drunk to avoid displeasing the gods. Indeed, two of the gods worshiped by Aztec tribes were believed to be perpetually intoxicated. Given the low alcohol content of their beverages and the strict control Indian civilizations exercised over drunkenness, it is unlikely that alcohol problems as we know them were common.

In the 1600s and 1700s, however, when Spanish traders appeared and introduced wine and spirits, this situation began to change. In combination with the conquest and destruction of the various Indian civilizations, the introduction of these new beverages altered the Indians' drinking patterns.

Pulque, a fermented beverage made from the juice of the agave plant, was popular in Mexico even before Columbus. Although pulque may be a valuable dietary supplement for the poor, providing vitamins, minerals, and protein, it is also capable of inflicting harm if consumed in large quantities.

European and American-type distilled beverages are used in virtually all countries in Latin America today. Even in the rural areas these beverages are now consumed as much as the traditional *chicha* and *pulque*. The major distilled alcohols of Latin America are mescal, tequila, and rum. Mescal and tequila are distilled from the agave cactus, yielding a colorless liquor of about 45% alcohol. When mescal is distilled from the peyote cactus, it is said to have a mild hallucinogenic effect. Mescal is sometimes called *aguardiente*, or "burnt water." Tequila is often drunk according to a ritual in which salt is sprinkled on the finger and licked clean just before swallowing a whole glass of the alcohol in a single gulp and biting into a wedge of lemon.

Rum, produced from the by-products of sugar cane mills in nearly all Caribbean countries, is perhaps the most powerful alcohol produced in Latin America, sometimes reaching a strength of 90% alcohol. In Peru *pisco*, a brandy, is considered the national drink.

Latin American countries differ considerably in their beverage preferences. Argentina and Chile have developed large wine industries and rank among the top ten wine-consuming nations of the world. In contrast, Mexico, Brazil, Colombia, Paraguay, and Venezuela are predominantly beer-drinking countries, although the average consumption is quite low in comparison to the European beer-drinking nations.

Although alcohol problems are reported to be widespread in Latin America, there is little evidence to support this. Compared with some of the European countries, however, the prevalence of cirrhosis of the liver is moderately high in Mexico, Chile, and Argentina. In most other Latin American countries alcohol-related diseases are less of a problem. Among the Camba, an Indian tribe living in eastern Bolivia, tremendous quantities of alcohol are consumed during regular weekend drinking bouts. According to custom, drinking is done at small social gatherings where each drinker offers toasts (*salud*) to the health of each of the other drinkers. Rapidly drinking glasses filled with 89% alcohol, the participants continue the ritual sequence until either all the alcohol is consumed or all the drinkers pass out. Although most members of the group typically drink themselves into a stupor, addiction to alcohol is rare.

The Indians of Tecospa, near Mexico City, offer another example of Latin American drinking practices. From the time of the Aztecs *pulque* has been considered a holy beverage and an integral part of their communal life. Pregnant women sometimes take an extra serving of *pulque* for "the one inside" them, and the dead are buried with tortillas and *pulque* to sustain them on their journey to the next world. Believing that *pulque* is a healthful drink that promotes harmony and contentment, they typically drink in groups of friends and family members. Drinking begins with ritual toasts and countertoasts, and often ends when most of the party collapses. In contrast to their nonviolent behavior during communal drinking, Tecospans often become involved in drunken disputes when they attend fairs and fiestas in the surrounding market towns.

The Urubu Indians of northern Brazil provide a more dramatic example of drinking among the Indians of Latin America. The Urubu drink a manioc (cassava) beer called *kau-i* ("crazy water"), which they believe contains a magical spirit that makes them crazy. In fact, in keeping with the name of the beer, the Urubu tend to lose their self-control when they are drunk, and violent quarrels sometimes break out at village feasts.

Drinking in Latin America, often explained in terms of the so-called cult of manliness (*el machismo*), is determined by how well one can hold one's liquor. Drunkenness is tolerated and even encouraged among men, though it is not considered proper for women to drink, especially in public. There are few restrictions on the production and sale of alcohol, reflecting a very tolerant attitude. This tolerance is exemplified by the complete abandonment that characterizes drinking during carnivals and other festival periods. At times such as just before the beginning of Lent, the whole community enters into a week-long period of outdoor celebration and uninhibited drinking.

Africa

Alcoholic beverages were known and used in Africa long before the beginning of European colonization. Beer was the most common beverage, prepared from cereal grains and, in East Africa, from bananas. Palm wine was and still is a common beverage in Nigeria. Distilled beverages such as gin and palm brandy are less common and more recent.

The traditional use of alcohol in Africa was closely linked with the economic and social events of the village, such as harvest celebrations, family feasts, and business agreements. In addition, beer was often an important part of the dowry the bridegroom had to pay the bride's family before a wedding could take place.

When the European colonizers arrived, alcohol assumed an important role as a trade commodity. Liquor, because it was inexpensive to produce and economical to transport, and firearms were traded for slaves, palm oil, ivory, and gold. With the introduction of distilled liquor, European drinking habits, such as drinking alcohol during meals, were superimposed on the native drinking customs. As Africa was divided among the French, Germans, English, Dutch, and Spanish, alcohol became an important source of tax revenue and was accepted in some colonies as a form of currency.

However, when Christian missionaries spread through Africa in the late 19th century, they brought with them the strong temperance philosophy of northern Europe and North America. As a result, a number of measures were adopted to stop the liquor trade with Africa. With the general decline of the temperance movement after the 1930s, the emerging independent nations of Africa began to establish local or nationalized facilities for the manufacture of alcoholic beverages to replace imports. Partly because of resentment against the colonial governments, past restrictions against the availability and use of alcohol were generally abandoned at the time of independence. Thus this new-found political freedom was often followed by a sharp increase in alcohol consumption, with European-style beverages, ironically, gaining an importance comparable to local beverages.

In Africa, consumption of the traditional beverages, beer and wine, has social, economic, and dietary functions. In many countries the very process of brewing beer is associated with different ceremonies. Until recently, beer was usually made in small quantities, which tended to be consumed by communal or family groups soon after fermentation. Home-produced beer or wine is consumed slowly with meals, often during a performance of some kind. Among the cattle-herding Bantu tribesmen of southern Africa, for example, beer plays an important part in both secular and religious rituals. Drinking is the principal attraction at almost every feast, the success of which is measured by the strength and quantity of the beer provided. Usually a communal drinking pot is passed from person to person or is placed in a rounded depression in the ground from which the beer is drawn with long-handled cups. With the men seated at one side and women on the other, each person drinks at a leisurely pace while the evening is passed in animated con-

The European colonization of Zaire brought with it the Protestant philosophy of temperance. For centuries locally produced beer has been consumed on special occasions in Zaire, but regular drinking is rare.

versation. While drunkenness and fighting are not uncommon during drinking episodes, alcoholism is considered rare in rural areas of Africa.

In contrast, the use of distilled liquor has been associated with drinking problems, especially in larger cities where increasing numbers of the rural population have migrated. With the increase in alcohol consumption and the breakdown of traditional social barriers against heavy drinking, drunkenness and alcoholism have begun to increase in the urban areas of countries such as Zambia and Nigeria. With the introduction of media advertising and aggressive marketing practices into these countries by multinational corporations, alcohol consumption is likely to increase.

Asia

The countries of Asia have not been noted for their alcohol consumption or production. In 1985 the Asiatic countries were among the lowest per capita consumers of alcohol, although drinking in Japan and South Korea has increased tremendously in recent years. However, wine has been used for thousands of years by the Chinese.

Among the people of ancient India, an intoxicating drink called *soma* was offered as a libation to the deities. Two countries, India and Japan, provide good examples of the drinking customs and rituals of contemporary Asia.

India To a great extent, attitudes toward alcohol have depended on Indian religious traditions. Both Hinduism and Islam, the two major religions of India, condemn the use of alcohol. There is considerably more tolerance for other intoxicants, such as opium and cannabis, in the areas dominated by these groups. During the colonial period the upper classes and the military adopted the drinking habits of the English, and traditional intoxicants were rejected in favor of gin, beer, and whiskey. During India's struggle for independence Mahatma Gandhi emphasized temperance as a means of protest against Western cultural influences. In fact, after independence was won in 1947, some parts of India imposed total prohibition.

In India drinking patterns vary according to gender, socioeconomic status, and region. One recent survey of drinking revealed that 42% of the men and 98% of the women have never had an alcoholic drink. The wealthy drink beer and foreign beverages (e.g., whiskey), while the poor drink mostly indigenous local liquors, which are often illegally distilled in the home. These home-produced beverages can be dangerous, causing blindness or even lethal poisoning when toxic industrial alcohol is substituted for ethyl alcohol. Drinking is more prevalent in the northwest and in the cities, while abstinence and prohibition are more typical of the Hindu areas. Although alcoholism is not unknown in India, it is practically nonexistent among females and compared to the industrialized countries is probably quite low even among males.

Japanese youth drinking beer and sake in front of a street-corner vending machine. As in South Korea and Hong Kong, economic prosperity in Japan has been associated with the substitution of western-style drinking practices for older traditional customs.

Japan In the 20th century, Japan has been transformed from a simple agricultural society to a modern industrialized nation. Though to a lesser extent, its drinking customs have also changed.

Unlike the Moslem or Christian nations, the dominant religions of Japan, Shintoism and Buddhism, exert little direct influence on drinking. Nevertheless, religious sanction is provided to the two national beverages, beer and *sake*, by linking them with religious ceremonies. (Sake is a rice wine, generally drunk hot, which has an average alcohol content of 15% to 16%.) For example, the local Shinto priest always conducts a series of purification ceremonies at each stage of the brewing cycle at the small sake breweries. The semi-

Many Tokyo restaurants serve snakes preserved in sake, claiming the reptiles are nutritious and promote sexual vigor. Such pairing of specific foods and drinks often evolved from folktales and remedies.

religious character of sake is also suggested in its use as a ceremonial offering to the divine powers.

Japan's cultural heritage is associated with another important aspect of its national drinking pattern: the social rituals surrounding alcohol use. Many of the ceremonial elements of social behavior among friends or acquaintances incorporate the use of sake. As a consequence, sake has acquired symbolic significance. Sake has also been connected to the rhythm of agricultural life. Rice, the most important agricultural product of Japan, is the principal ingredient of sake. The same pride and care that goes into rice growing is extended during the winter to the laborious brewing process. Thus, despite the dramatic changes taking place in

American war correspondents drink with a Japanese major in Shanghai in 1945, one month after Japan's unconditional surrender. Sharing a drink is universally seen as a gesture of friendship and equality.

Japanese society, these practices persist in linking contemporary culture with the past.

In comparison to the other nations of the world, Japan is considered to be a country of moderate drinkers and abstainers. Daily alcohol consumption is considered unusual, as is drinking by women, and drinking among males occurs primarily in social settings. Both at weekend outings with friends and business meetings with associates, sake drinking is surrounded by many ceremonies and by expectations of bringing solidarity, togetherness, and harmony. On certain occasions, it is acceptable to become intoxicated, but the rules of social intercourse demand that correct behavior be maintained within acceptable limits. Although solitary drink-

In Japan, sake is linked with religious ceremonies. Rice, from which sake is brewed, historically has been one of this country's major foods, grown with great pride and care. Because of this, sake has become linked with the rhythms of agricultural life.

ing is not condemned, it is likely to be considered deviant.

In the rural fishing community of Takashima, for example, feasts and weddings are occasions for heavy drinking by the men. After a banquet liberally complemented with various alcoholic beverages, drinking continues during song and dance performances. Although drunkenness occurs, there is little fighting or boisterous behavior. The annual autumn festival is another occasion for heavy drinking, especially by the young, unmarried men of the village. After a tipsy procession in which the village's portable religious shrine is paraded, the males continue their drinking into the evening without risk of being reprimanded by their elders.

In recent years, drinking patterns have begun to change in Japan. Since 1960 there has been a steady increase in alcohol consumption, primarily of beer, whiskey, and brandy. Today Japan is both a beer-drinking and a wine-drinking nation. More women are now drinking and there is a growing concern with the connection between drinking and traffic accidents. Specialized treatment facilities for alcoholics date only from 1975, suggesting that alcohol has only recently been recognized as a health problem.

The Middle East and North Africa

No discussion of drinking customs in Africa and Asia can be complete without considering the influence of Islam. The prophet Mohammed founded the religion in Arabia in the 7th century. Islam spread rapidly westward through Egypt and North Africa, and to the east through what is now Iraq, Iran, Afghanistan, India, and Indonesia. Today it is the predominant religion in more than thirty countries, and exerts a major influence in the lives of over one-sixth of the world's population. Of all the countries of the world, the Moslem nations are usually and justly regarded as the most abstemious regarding alcoholic beverages. Except for the vineyards planted in Algeria by the French, practically no alcohol is produced in these countries, and little alcohol is sold or consumed.

What accounts for this remarkable degree of temperance among the Moslems is the Koran, Islam's most sacred book of scriptures. The early followers of Mohammed interpreted the Koran as absolutely prohibiting the use of alcoholic beverages, except in cases of extreme thirst or sickness.

This prohibition has been enforced with various degrees of success in different countries. In the most orthodox Moslem countries, such as Saudi Arabia, alcohol is considered the "mother of vices," and drinking and especially intoxication are treated by corporal punishment. Even non-Moslem foreign visitors have been flogged for liquor-related offenses, such as the illegal making of alcohol. By rendering drinking immoral and alcohol production illegal, Islam has effectively prevented drinking and alcohol-related problems for over a thousand years.

Staff members of the Iranian embassy dispose of liquor stocks after Ayatollah Khomeini's overthrow of the shah's government. With the revival of religious fundamentalism in the Moslem countries of the Middle East, western-style drinking customs are being eliminated, as is the general availability of alcoholic beverages.

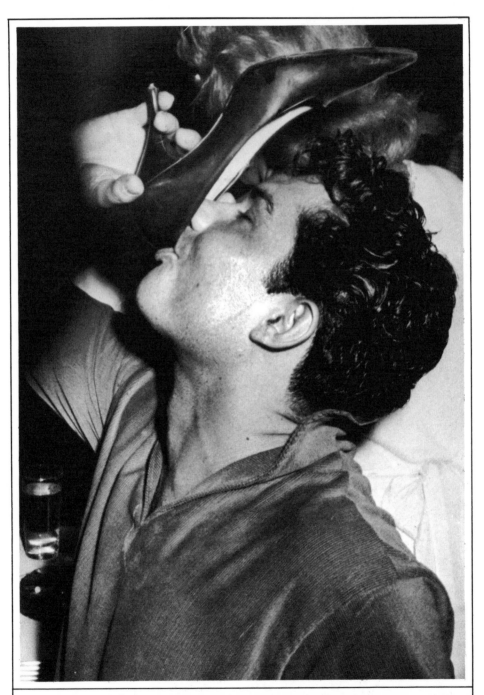

Caught up in a festive atmosphere, a dancer drinks from the slipper of his dancing partner. The loss of inhibitions that often accompanies alcohol use can result in erratic or dangerous behavior.

CHAPTER 5

DRINKING
IN THE 1980s

What accounts for the tremendous differences in drinking customs among societies and between ethnic groups around the world? Drinking customs are not static, but rather evolve out of circumstances dictated by technological development, geography, economics, and cultural factors. Advances in technology, which determine the ease with which brewing, fermentation, and distillation are conducted, played an important role in the tremendous increase in alcohol production during the 19th and 20th centuries. Geography affects alcohol production in that soil conditions and climate differ greatly from area to area and thus determine what agriculture is possible. Historically, people drank what was produced locally, and local production depended on the availability of fruits, grains, and other products.

Economic factors affect drinking customs by limiting availability to those who can afford alcoholic beverages. Relatively inexpensive beverages such as wine and beer are used by the middle and lower classes, while the more expensive champagnes and distilled beverages are incorporated into the lifestyles of the rich. Despite the common belief that legal controls on alcohol's availability do little to influence drinking, in fact, it is clear that laws do have a definite effect on drinking customs and alcohol problems. Tax policies have kept alcohol consumption low in the Scandinavian countries, and in the course of a few years they have changed the beverage of preference from spirits to beer in Belgium and Denmark.

When a beverage is closely identified with the history and economic welfare of a nation, as wine is with France and Italy, drinking customs become a source of patriotic pride. And when drinking is sanctioned by the dominant religion of a group, drinking customs and rituals are greatly influenced. In Moslem countries, no drinking customs exist because abstinence is the rule. Among the Jews, because wine and spirits are closely integrated into religious rituals, drinking in moderation is most common. And in Catholic countries, excessive alcohol use and complex drinking customs are in part attributable to the Church's traditional

At the Jewish Passover Seder, as each of the ten plagues is mentioned a drop of wine is removed from the glass to remind the participants not only of God's punishment but of the enemy's suffering.

Table 2

Alcohol-Related Problem Rates in Representative European Countries				
INTERNATIONAL RANK IN PER CAPITA CONSUMPTION	COUNTRY	DEATHS FROM LIVER CIRRHOSIS*	DRUNKEN-NESS-ARRESTS**	% ALCOHOL-RELATED FATAL ACCIDENTS
8	Switzerland	20.4	N/A	19.2%
21	The Netherlands	8.0	.02	N/A
25	Poland	18.0	1.65	30.0%
26	Ireland	5.7	.22	N/A
30	Finland	10.1	7.49	23.0%

* Cirrhosis mortality per 100,000 persons 25 years or older, 1975 figures
** Rate of Public Drunkenness arrests per 1,000 persons 15 years or older, 1975 figures
*** Percent of all traffic accidents where a fatality was attributed to alcohol
N/A Data not available

association with the production of alcohol.

In modern times two new factors have emerged as major determinants of drinking customs: the concentration of production in multinational corporations, and the internationalization of drinking practices through advertising and social modeling. The increasing use of sophisticated advertising techniques to market alcoholic beverages has greatly encouraged the adoption of new drinking practices by youth and women, especially in developing nations.

Because of the extent to which technological innovation, geography, religion, and history differ among societies, one should not be surprised by the tremendous variety of beverage preferences, drinking patterns, and alcohol-related behaviors. Some groups, like the Italians, favor dietary uses. Other groups, like the Finns, drink primarily for the intoxicating effects of alcohol. Still other groups, the French for example, have developed customs that support practically every possible usage of alcohol.

Although there is some evidence to suggest that the Chinese and other Asian groups have a biological sensitivity to alcohol that causes them to become flushed and even nauseous when drinking, this did not prevent a dramatic increase in drinking among the Japanese, Koreans, and Chinese-Americans during the 1970s, nor does it explain why the peoples of Africa, India, and the Middle East, who do not exhibit this sensitivity, are the most temperate in the world. Clearly social and cultural factors greatly affect the development and regulation of drinking customs.

Despite the diversity of drinking practices around the world and throughout history, there is, nevertheless, a remarkable degree of similarity in the ways people use alcoholic beverages. These similarities can be summarized in terms of six different functions of drinking customs: medicinal, religious, social, recreational, dietary, and symbolic. Almost all societies attribute healing qualities to alcohol, especially wine and spirits. Numerous folk remedies pre-

Orioles' players get a champagne bath in the clubhouse following a pennant-winning victory. Champagne, the most lively and one of the most expensive quality wines, has become linked with celebrations.

scribe the use of alcohol for the cure of disease or relief from pain. The religious functions of drinking are evident in the rituals developed by some of the world's major religious groups. Not only is wine incorporated into the holiest ceremonies of the Catholic and Jewish religions, festival drinking still occurs in many Catholic countries in connection with Lenten season.

The social, recreational, and dietary functions of drinking customs are numerous. Hospitality customs dictate that certain alcoholic beverages be offered to guests. Social customs prescribe who drinks and how much is consumed. Recreational customs influence when (e.g., after work, on Friday night) and where (e.g., at a bar, or a party) people drink. In almost all societies, these informal social rules allow men to drink more often than women, and in greater amounts per occasion. Ceremonies and social rituals such as toasting, drinking healths, and buying rounds give meaning

A bride and groom share bread and wine with a priest during their wedding. This ancient rite of the Roman Catholic church was recently revised so that churchgoers could participate more directly in the Mass.

and structure to the drinking occasion.

Finally, one should not underestimate the symbolic functions of drinking customs. Advertisers are aware of the symbolic value of premium beers, fine wines, and expensive whiskeys. Both the choice of alcoholic beverage and the way in which it is consumed communicate a great deal about the personality and tastes of the drinker, or at least about the image the drinker would like to present to the world. Men may learn to project a "macho" image by drinking a certain beer, while women may communicate an air of sophistication by ordering an exotic drink or special wine. In a similar way, abstinence from alcohol symbolizes something about the moral or religious convictions of people, be they Moslem, Methodist, or recovering alcoholics.

Not only do drinking customs influence how and why people drink, they also contribute to the problems experienced during and after the ingestion of alcohol. One of the greatest problems all societies have encountered since antiquity is drunkenness, that is, the behavior of people when they drink excessively. What is striking about our description of different drinking cultures is the great variety of ways inebriation is expressed. The Japanese tend to become sociable and friendly when drunk; the Camba of Bolivia pass out, and the Finns often become boisterous and argumentative.

Just as culture teaches the members of a society the customs and rituals surrounding alcohol use, culture also teaches the drinker how to behave while drunk. In many cultures, being drunk is considered "time out" from the demands of society. Bizarre or obnoxious behavior, unthinkable under normal circumstances, is often tolerated because the person is thought to be drunk and therefore not responsible. While most people believe that the conscience is soluble in alcohol, it appears that this is true only in societies where custom leads people to interpret their intoxication as an excuse for irresponsibility or revelry. Alcohol is not the only culprit, and perhaps not the most important one.

But drunkenness is only one of many consequences that result from drinking. Countries differ significantly in the extent of problems associated with alcohol (see Table 1). Deaths from liver cirrhosis, a common complication of chronic drinking, are high in wine-drinking Switzerland but low in beer-drinking Ireland. The spirits-drinking Finns have a relatively low rate of cirrhosis mortality but an extremely high rate of arrests for public drunkenness. Although these arrests are low among the vodka-drinking Poles, in this country fatal accidents involving alcohol are relatively high. However, international statistics are not always reliable, and they often reflect as much about the record-keeping habits of a country than they do about drinking habits. Nevertheless, it is likely that habitual drinking customs contribute to the high cirrhosis rates among the wine-drinking countries, as well as the problems, such as drunkenness arrests, associated with acute intoxication in countries where drinking is more sporadic.

The example of antiquity indicates that drinking becomes problematic under several circumstances: (1) when simple nomadic or rural peoples change their style of living after moving to urban environments; (2) when occasional ceremonial drinking shifts to regular tavern drinking by the general urban populations; (3) when alcohol is first introduced to primitive peoples, such as the Gauls, Germans, and American Indians; and (4) when increasing wealth and rising standards of living make alcohol more available.

The ancient civilizations did not view drunkenness or alcohol dependence as serious problems for health or public order. Therefore, there was little legislation controlling drinking and few popular movements to advocate abstinence. Alcohol use only became problematic on an international scale during the past 200 years. As drinking continues to increase among the world's population, it is likely that drinking problems will continue to grow in those societies where heavy drinking customs predominate.

In 1635 Thomas Dekker said: "To drink healths is to drink sickness." The drinking of healths and many other drinking customs do indeed have the potential for causing damage, but they also serve a variety of social and psychological functions that bring enjoyment to the millions of drinkers who use alcohol without problems. The real challenge for all societies is to develop and encourage drinking customs that allow people to enjoy alcoholic beverages (or to feel free to refuse them), while minimizing the negative consequences that have plagued civilization since the discovery of fermentation.

APPENDIX 1

		INTER-NATIONAL RANK	LITERS OF ABSOLUTE ALCOHOL			
AREA	COUNTRY		WINE	BEER	SPIRITS	TOTAL
EUROPE	France	1	11.6	2.9	2.3	16.8
	Italy	2	11.1	.6	1.9	13.6
	Austria	3	4.1	6.0	2.3	12.4
	Portugal	4	9.9	.8	1.0	11.7
	Luxembourg	5	5.0	3.7	2.8	11.5
	Spain	6	7.1	1.4	2.9	11.4
	West Germany	7	2.3	5.8	2.9	11.0
	Switzerland	8	5.0	3.8	2.1	10.8
	Hungary	10	4.4	2.0	3.1	9.5
	Belgium	11	1.9	5.8	1.6	9.3
	Czechoslovakia	12	1.1	4.5	2.4	8.6
	Denmark	15	.9	5.3	1.5	7.7
	Yugoslavia	16	3.2	1.7	2.8	7.7
	Great Britain	18	.5	5.3	1.1	6.9
	East Germany	20	.7	3.2	2.9	6.8
	Netherlands	21	.8	3.3	2.3	6.4
	Soviet Union	23	2.0	.9	3.4	6.3
	Bulgaria	24	2.4	1.9	1.8	6.1
	Poland	25	.8	1.3	3.9	6.0
	Ireland	26	.5	3.8	1.7	6.0
	Sweden	27	1.0	2.1	2.7	5.8
	Greece	29	4.8	.5	.1	5.4
	Finland	30	.6	2.2	2.3	5.1
	Norway	34	.4	1.8	1.6	3.8
	Roumania	35	2.6		1.2	3.8
	Iceland	39	.2	.2	2.4	2.8
UNITED STATES & OTHER ENGLISH-SPEAKING COUNTRIES	Australia	13	1.1	6.3	1.1	8.5
	New Zealand	14	.9	6.1	1.2	8.2
	Canada	17	.9	4.1	2.6	7.6
	United States	19	.8	3.0	3.0	6.8
ASIA	Japan	28	2.8	1.6	1.1	5.5
	South Korea	32		.7	3.5	4.2
	Cyprus	33	1.2	.9	1.8	3.9
	Hong Kong	46		.6	1.2	1.8
LATIN AMERICA	Argentina	9	9.5	.7		10.2
	Chile	22	5.3	1.1		6.4
	Uruguay	31	3.1	1.5		4.6
	Surinam	36		1.1	2.5	3.6
	Panama	38		1.3	1.6	2.9
	Peru	40	.2	1.0	1.4	2.6
	Mexico	41		1.4	1.1	2.5
	Cuba	42	.2	1.0	1.3	2.5
	Bolivia	43		.4	1.7	2.1
	Venezuela	44		2.1		2.1
	Brazil	52	.1	.5	.2	.7
	Paraguay	54	.2	.3		.5

Average Yearly Consumption of Wine, Beer, and Spirits Per Person in 62 Countries

Average Yearly Consumption of Wine, Beer, and Spirits Per Person in 62 Countries

AREA	COUNTRY	INTER-NATIONAL RANK	LITERS OF ABSOLUTE ALCOHOL			TOTAL
			WINE	BEER	SPIRITS	
AFRICA	South Africa	37	1.2	.7	1.0	2.9
	Cameroon	48		.9		.9
	Namibia	49		.9		.9
	Congo	50		.7		.7
	Kenya	56		.4		.4
	Senegal	57	.1	.2		.3
	Gambia	60	.1	.1		.2
MIDDLE EAST & MOSLEM COUNTRIES	Bahrain	45	.1	.7	1.3	2.1
	Israel	47	.5	.5	.7	1.7
	Tunisia	51	.4	.3		.7
	Turkey	53	.1		.4	.5
	Lebanon	55	.4			.4
	Algeria	58	.1	.2		.3
	Morocco	59	.2	.1		.3
	Egypt	61			.1	.1
	Syria	62			.1	.1

SOURCE: 1972 survey by the Finnish Foundation of Alcohol Studies and World Health Organization.

To your health!
Salud!
Prosit!
A vôtre santé!
Kan pei!
Skål!
Terveydeksi!
Stin ygia sou!
Slainthe is saol agat!
L'chaim!
Alla tua salute!
Kwa afya yako!
Op je gezonheid!
Na zdrowie!
Za vashe z-dorovye!
Viva!
Ziveli!
Iechyd da i chivri!
I sveikata!
Egeszsegedre!

The drinking of "healths" is one of the oldest and most universal drinking customs, as reflected in the many languages in which this toast appears.

APPENDIX 2

STATE AGENCIES FOR THE PREVENTION AND TREATMENT OF DRUG ABUSE

ALABAMA
Department of Mental Health
Division of Mental Illness and
  Substance Abuse Community
  Programs
200 Interstate Park Drive
P.O. Box 3710
Montgomery, AL 36193
(205) 271-9253

ALASKA
Department of Health and Social
  Services
Office of Alcoholism and Drug
  Abuse
Pouch H-05-F
Juneau, AK 99811
(907) 586-6201

ARIZONA
Department of Health Services
Division of Behavioral Health
  Services
Bureau of Community Services
Alcohol Abuse and Alcoholism
  Section
2500 East Van Buren
Phoenix, AZ 85008
(602) 255-1238

Department of Health Services
Division of Behavioral Health
  Services
Bureau of Community Services
Drug Abuse Section
2500 East Van Buren
Phoenix, AZ 85008
(602) 255-1240

ARKANSAS
Department of Human Services
Office on Alcohol and Drug Abuse
  Prevention
1515 West 7th Avenue
Suite 310
Little Rock, AR 72202
(501) 371-2603

CALIFORNIA
Department of Alcohol and Drug
  Abuse
111 Capitol Mall
Sacramento, CA 95814
(916) 445-1940

COLORADO
Department of Health
Alcohol and Drug Abuse Division
4210 East 11th Avenue
Denver, CO 80220
(303) 320-6137

CONNECTICUT
Alcohol and Drug Abuse
  Commission
999 Asylum Avenue
3rd Floor
Hartford, CT 06105
(203) 566-4145

DELAWARE
Division of Mental Health
Bureau of Alcoholism and Drug
  Abuse
1901 North Dupont Highway
Newcastle, DE 19720
(302) 421-6101

DISTRICT OF COLUMBIA
Department of Human Services
Office of Health Planning and
  Development
601 Indiana Avenue, NW
Suite 500
Washington, D.C. 20004
(202) 724-5641

FLORIDA
Department of Health and
  Rehabilitative Services
Alcoholic Rehabilitation Program
1317 Winewood Boulevard
Room 187A
Tallahassee, FL 32301
(904) 488-0396

Department of Health and
  Rehabilitative Services
Drug Abuse Program
1317 Winewood Boulevard
Building 6, Room 155
Tallahassee, FL 32301
(904) 488-0900

GEORGIA
Department of Human Resources
Division of Mental Health and
  Mental Retardation
Alcohol and Drug Section
618 Ponce De Leon Avenue, NE
Atlanta, GA 30365-2101
(404) 894-4785

HAWAII
Department of Health
Mental Health Division
Alcohol and Drug Abuse Branch
1250 Punch Bowl Street
P.O. Box 3378
Honolulu, HI 96801
(808) 548-4280

IDAHO
Department of Health and Welfare
Bureau of Preventive Medicine
Substance Abuse Section
450 West State
Boise, ID 83720
(208) 334-4368

ILLINOIS
Department of Mental Health and
  Developmental Disabilities
Division of Alcoholism
160 North La Salle Street
Room 1500
Chicago, IL 60601
(312) 793-2907

Illinois Dangerous Drugs
  Commission
300 North State Street
Suite 1500
Chicago, IL 60610
(312) 822-9860

INDIANA
Department of Mental Health
Division of Addiction Services
429 North Pennsylvania Street
Indianapolis, IN 46204
(317) 232-7816

IOWA
Department of Substance Abuse
505 5th Avenue
Insurance Exchange Building
Suite 202
Des Moines, IA 50319
(515) 281-3641

KANSAS
Department of Social Rehabilitation
Alcohol and Drug Abuse Services
2700 West 6th Street
Biddle Building
Topeka, KS 66606
(913) 296-3925

KENTUCKY
Cabinet for Human Resources
Department of Health Services
Substance Abuse Branch
275 East Main Street
Frankfort, KY 40601
(502) 564-2880

LOUISIANA
Department of Health and Human
  Resources
Office of Mental Health and
  Substance Abuse
655 North 5th Street
P.O. Box 4049
Baton Rouge, LA 70821
(504) 342-2565

MAINE
Department of Human Services
Office of Alcoholism and Drug
  Abuse Prevention
Bureau of Rehabilitation
32 Winthrop Street
Augusta, ME 04330
(207) 289-2781

MARYLAND
Alcoholism Control Administration
201 West Preston Street
Fourth Floor
Baltimore, MD 21201
(301) 383-2977

State Health Department
Drug Abuse Administration
201 West Preston Street
Baltimore, MD 21201
(301) 383-3312

MASSACHUSETTS
Department of Public Health
Division of Alcoholism
755 Boylston Street
Sixth Floor
Boston, MA 02116
(617) 727-1960

Department of Public Health
Division of Drug Rehabilitation
600 Washington Street
Boston, MA 02114
(617) 727-8617

MICHIGAN
Department of Public Health
Office of Substance Abuse Services
3500 North Logan Street
P.O. Box 30035
Lansing, MI 48909
(517) 373-8603

MINNESOTA
Department of Public Welfare
Chemical Dependency Program
  Division
Centennial Building
658 Cedar Street
4th Floor
Saint Paul, MN 55155
(612) 296-4614

MISSISSIPPI
Department of Mental Health
Division of Alcohol and Drug Abuse
1102 Robert E. Lee Building
Jackson, MS 39201
(601) 359-1297

MISSOURI
Department of Mental Health
Division of Alcoholism and Drug
  Abuse
2002 Missouri Boulevard
P.O. Box 687
Jefferson City, MO 65102
(314) 751-4942

MONTANA
Department of Institutions
Alcohol and Drug Abuse Division
1539 11th Avenue
Helena, MT 59620
(406) 449-2827

NEBRASKA
Department of Public Institutions
Division of Alcoholism and Drug Abuse
801 West Van Dorn Street
P.O. Box 94728
Lincoln, NB 68509
(402) 471-2851, Ext. 415

NEVADA
Department of Human Resources
Bureau of Alcohol and Drug Abuse
505 East King Street
Carson City, NV 89710
(702) 885-4790

NEW HAMPSHIRE
Department of Health and Welfare
Office of Alcohol and Drug Abuse
  Prevention
Hazen Drive
Health and Welfare Building
Concord, NH 03301
(603) 271-4627

NEW JERSEY
Department of Health
Division of Alcoholism
129 East Hanover Street CN 362
Trenton, NJ 08625
(609) 292-8949

Department of Health
Division of Narcotic and Drug Abuse
  Control
129 East Hanover Street CN 362
Trenton, NJ 08625
(609) 292-8949

NEW MEXICO
Health and Environment Department
Behavioral Services Division
Substance Abuse Bureau
725 Saint Michaels Drive
P.O. Box 968
Santa Fe, NM 87503
(505) 984-0020, Ext. 304

NEW YORK
Division of Alcoholism and Alcohol
  Abuse
194 Washington Avenue
Albany, NY 12210
(518) 474-5417

Division of Substance Abuse
  Services
Executive Park South
Box 8200
Albany, NY 12203
(518) 457-7629

NORTH CAROLINA
Department of Human Resources
Division of Mental Health, Mental
  Retardation and Substance Abuse
  Services
Alcohol and Drug Abuse Services
325 North Salisbury Street
Albemarle Building
Raleigh, NC 27611
(919) 733-4670

NORTH DAKOTA
Department of Human Services
Division of Alcoholism and Drug
  Abuse
State Capitol Building
Bismarck, ND 58505
(701) 224-2767

OHIO
Department of Health
Division of Alcoholism
246 North High Street
P.O. Box 118
Columbus, OH 43216
(614) 466-3543

Department of Mental Health
Bureau of Drug Abuse
65 South Front Street
Columbus, OH 43215
(614) 466-9023

OKLAHOMA
Department of Mental Health
Alcohol and Drug Programs
4545 North Lincoln Boulevard
Suite 100 East Terrace
P.O. Box 53277
Oklahoma City, OK 73152
(405) 521-0044

OREGON
Department of Human Resources
Mental Health Division
Office of Programs for Alcohol and
  Drug Problems
2575 Bittern Street, NE
Salem, OR 97310
(503) 378-2163

PENNSYLVANIA
Department of Health
Office of Drug and Alcohol
  Programs
Commonwealth and Forster Avenues
Health and Welfare Building
P.O. Box 90
Harrisburg, PA 17108
(717) 787-9857

RHODE ISLAND
Department of Mental Health,
  Mental Retardation and Hospitals
Division of Substance Abuse
Substance Abuse Administration
  Building
Cranston, RI 02920
(401) 464-2091

SOUTH CAROLINA
Commission on Alcohol and Drug
  Abuse
3700 Forest Drive
Columbia, SC 29204
(803) 758-2521

SOUTH DAKOTA
Department of Health
Division of Alcohol and Drug Abuse
523 East Capitol, Joe Foss Building
Pierre, SD 57501
(605) 773-4806

TENNESSEE
Department of Mental Health and
  Mental Retardation
Alcohol and Drug Abuse Services
505 Deaderick Street
James K. Polk Building, Fourth Floor
Nashville, TN 37219
(615) 741-1921

TEXAS
Commission on Alcoholism
809 Sam Houston State Office Building
Austin, TX 78701
(512) 475-2577

Department of Community Affairs
Drug Abuse Prevention Division
2015 South Interstate Highway 35
P.O. Box 13166
Austin, TX 78711
(512) 443-4100

UTAH
Department of Social Services
Division of Alcoholism and Drugs
150 West North Temple
Suite 350
P.O. Box 2500
Salt Lake City, UT 84110
(801) 533-6532

VERMONT
Agency of Human Services
Department of Social and
  Rehabilitation Services
Alcohol and Drug Abuse Division
103 South Main Street
Waterbury, VT 05676
(802) 241-2170

VIRGINIA
Department of Mental Health and
  Mental Retardation
Division of Substance Abuse
109 Governor Street
P.O. Box 1797
Richmond, VA 23214
(804) 786-5313

WASHINGTON
Department of Social and Health
  Service
Bureau of Alcohol and Substance
  Abuse
Office Building—44 W
Olympia, WA 98504
(206) 753-5866

WEST VIRGINIA
Department of Health
Office of Behavioral Health Services
Division on Alcoholism and Drug
  Abuse
1800 Washington Street East
Building 3 Room 451
Charleston, WV 25305
(304) 348-2276

WISCONSIN
Department of Health and Social
  Services
Division of Community Services
Bureau of Community Programs
Alcohol and Other Drug Abuse
  Program Office
1 West Wilson Street
P.O. Box 7851
Madison, WI 53707
(608) 266-2717

WYOMING
Alcohol and Drug Abuse Programs
Hathaway Building
Cheyenne, WY 82002
(307) 777-7115, Ext. 7118

GUAM
Mental Health & Substance Abuse
  Agency
P.O. Box 20999
Guam 96921

PUERTO RICO
Department of Addiction Control
  Services
Alcohol Abuse Programs
P.O. Box B-Y Rio Piedras Station
Rio Piedras, PR 00928
(809) 763-5014

Department of Addiction Control
  Services
Drug Abuse Programs
P.O. Box B-Y Rio Piedras Station
Rio Piedras, PR 00928
(809) 764-8140

VIRGIN ISLANDS
Division of Mental Health,
  Alcoholism & Drug Dependency
  Services
P.O. Box 7329
Saint Thomas, Virgin Islands 00801
(809) 774-7265

AMERICAN SAMOA
LBJ Tropical Medical Center
Department of Mental Health Clinic
Pago Pago, American Samoa 96799

TRUST TERRITORIES
Director of Health Services
Office of the High Commissioner
Saipan, Trust Territories 96950

Further Reading

Armyr, G., Elmer, A. and Herz, U. *Alcohol in the World of the 80s. Habits, Attitudes, Preventive Policies and Voluntary Efforts.* Stockholm: Sober Forlags, 1982.

Austin, G. A. *Perspectives on the History of Psychoactive Substance Use.* Washington, D.C.: U.S. Government Printing Office, 1978.

Cahalan, D., Cisin, I. H. and Crossley, H. M. *American Drinking Practices.* New Brunswick, N J: Rutgers Center of Alcohol Studies, 1969.

Clark, N. H. *Deliver us from Evil: An Interpretation of American Prohibition.* New York: Norton, 1976.

Hastings, D. *Spirits and Liquors of the World.* Hong Kong: Chartwell Books, 1984.

Lender, M. E. and Martin, J. K. *Drinking in America: A History.* New York: Free Press, 1982.

MacAndrew, C. and Edgerton, R. B. *Drunken Comportment: A Social Explanation.* Chicago: Aldine, 1969.

Makela, K., Room, R., Single, E., Sulkunen, P. and Walsh, B. *Alcohol, Society, and the State.* Toronto: Addiction Research Foundation, 1981.

Marshall, M., ed. *Beliefs, Behaviors, and Alcoholic Beverages: A Cross-Cultural Survey.* Ann Arbor, MI: University of Michigan Press, 1979.

Pittman, D. J. and Snyder, C. R. *Society, Culture and Drinking Patterns.* New York: John Wiley, 1962.

Index

Thomas Babor, Ph.D., obtained his degree in social psychology from the University of Arizona. He received his M.S. in psychiatric epidemiology from Harvard University's School of Public Health. He has been an assistant professor in the department of psychiatry at the Harvard Medical School. Currently he is associate director of the Alcohol Research Center at the University of Connecticut's School of Medicine, where he is also an associate professor in the department of psychiatry.

Solomon H. Snyder, M.D., is Distinguished Service Professor of Neuroscience, Pharmacology and Psychiatry at The Johns Hopkins University School of Medicine. He has served as president of the Society for Neuroscience and in 1978 received the Albert Laster Award in Medical Research. He has authored *Uses of Marijuana, Madness and the Brain, The Troubled Mind, Biological Aspects of Mental Disorder,* and edited *Perspective in Neuropharmacology: A Tribute to Julius Axelrod.* Professor Snyder was a research associate with Dr. Axelrod at the National Institutes of Health.

Barry L. Jacobs, Ph.D., is currently a professor in the program of neuroscience at Princeton University. Professor Jacobs is author of *Serotonin Neurotransmission and Behavior* and *Hallucinogens: Neurochemical, Behavioral and Clinical Perspectives.* He has written many journal articles in the field of neuroscience and contributed numerous chapters to books on behavior and brain science. He has been a member of several panels of the National Institute of Mental Health.

Jerome H. Jaffe, M.D., formerly professor of psychiatry at the College of Physicians and Surgeons, Columbia University, has been named recently Director of the Addiction Research Center of the National Institute on Drug Abuse. Dr. Jaffe is also a psychopharmacologist and has conducted research on a wide range of addictive drugs and developed treatment programs for addicts. He has acted as Special Consultant to the President on Narcotics and Dangerous Drugs and was the first director of the White House Special Action Office for Drug Abuse Prevention.